Foreword

When I first met Danny and Darci Cahill it was after the *Biggest Loser* season that Danny was on had already ended and mutual friends introduced us at a dinner party in their honor. They are a good looking couple with vibrant smiles and I found them to be very warm, kind, easy to talk to, and comfortable to be around. I loved them immediately. I would never have dreamed by looking at them, and talking with them, that they had gone through all that they have in their lives.

After dinner we listened as Danny talked about his life story, and then Darci added some of her own life experience and perspective as well, and I was completely amazed that they were not only still standing, but standing in triumph. And I am not talking about just the weight issues Danny struggled with for years—as difficult as that was, and for completely understandable reasons—I am talking about the serious, multiple problems that Danny and Darci each faced alone in themselves and together as a couple, any one of which could have destroyed a lesser man or woman, as well as their marriage.

The painful things Danny suffered could not bring down the indomitable spirit he was born with. One heartbreaking situation after another could not destroy Darci, who became through it all a faithful woman of God and a prayer warrior for her husband. They hung on when most people wouldn't have. They are survivors in every sense of the word. Now, they are an encouragement—for anyone who faces tough struggles—to never give up.

From gut-wrenching to inspiring, this story will touch anyone who reads it. When I read this book I couldn't put it down. I loved it. They are painfully honest in their writing, as only two people can be whose lives have been completely transformed by God and have come out whole on the other side of it all. They now know where their strength comes from. I'm sure you will love their story, too. It will be an encouragement to everyone who enjoys uplifting true stories assuring us that we, too, can have victory in life. And I believe you will come to love them as well. Danny and Darci are now the biggest winners you will ever know.

—Stormie Omartian*

*Best selling author of The Power of a Praying series, which included The Power of a Praying Wife, The Power of a Praying Husband, The Power of a Praying Woman, and Just Enough Light For the Step I'm On. Over 17 million books sold.

Table of Contents

Darci's Acknowledgements:

First of all, I want to thank my Lord and Savior Jesus Christ, without Him life and love would be impossible and without Hope. To this day, I am amazed at the people God has joined to me to make this life incredible. Danny you are a champion and my greatest treasure. My wish for you "is that this life becomes ALL that you want it too!" I am truly the luckiest woman in the world because I have you. David, my Son, thank you for always making me smile; God has BIG plans for you. I can't wait to see you make the world a better place. Mary Claire, you were my heart's desire and my best mother's day gift ever! You are sunshine wherever you go. Never lose your desire to do what is right. Thank you to my Mom, Beverly, there will never be enough words to express my love and gratitude. Thank you for seeing the best in everyone you meet, you are truly a picture of God's grace. To my Dad, thank you, I know I can always count on you to be there for me and my family. My siblings Rock!! Dacri and Bob, Dan and Julie, thank you…..Dan, a special thanks for hauling away all that junk! Bob the deck was incredible… It looked so good it made it on NBC! Sweetheart, thank you for always doing whatever needed to be done, I love you. To my peeps, Tammie, Kathy, Michelle, Kristin …seriously powerful women of God!! Your prayers "availed much!!" Not to mention all of the help your families gave with my kids while Danny was at the ranch. Marsha Pogue, thank you for being my trainer – but most of all, thank you for becoming my friend. You are priceless. Sherry King, thanks for the idea of "The Biggest Loser", I hope you know you were hearing the Lord. Arthur and Noell Greeno, you are Rock Stars! Thank you for putting together the army of people that made this "champion moment" a reality. To the countless numbers of people that gave money and resources, may you be richly blessed. God is good, all the time!

Danny's Acknowledgements:

First, a special thank you to God, who saw in me what I didn't, and in special ways – day by day - revealed your glory, or worth, to me. Thank you to Darci; without you, my life wouldn't only be boring, but empty. You filled a whole in my heart that only you could. I am truly blessed by you. David, you are such a champion. In your weakest moment you showed me that no matter the circumstance, you've got to trust God. That lesson you taught me in the hospital that day not only made be believe I wasn't a failure as a father, but since then every day that I've needed God, I've called on him. Mary Claire, I know of no other person in the world full of more love than you. I think there is so much you can't contain it! Be sure to save some of that love for yourself. To my Mother, who taught me that I was strong. Because of your love and care, so many people in the world have been blessed. Your selflessness shows the Love of Christ every day! To my sister Cathy, who taught me to read, to strive, and to sweep the house or else! We are so alike it's scary – and awesome. My sister Charla, who always gave me a reason to smile! Never was there a day growing up when you didn't say something that made me so glad you were with me.

To my Grandpa Charlie – I never knew you very well, and I felt robbed of our relationship, but those things you did give me were priceless. To my Church, Orlando and Kim Juarez, and to all of my friends (especially Noell & Arthur Greeno!) who all came together to hold us up and cradle us through the journey when we needed it most. To Marsha Pogue for keeping me in tip-top shape, and Miranda Burcham who was my "Jillian home!" You told me you felt you were supposed to be on the show, and when I stood on that scale and won, you were! To Grandma Ada, who loved me no matter what! And to my dad, Charlie. You didn't tell me what a champion was; you showed me! Thank you for showing me that sometimes you just gotta do what has to be done…because it's the right thing to do! I miss you so much and can't wait to see you again.

"Grandpa, what was the war like?"

"Well son, it was a little bit of hell, a little bit of fun, a little bit of excitement, a little boring at times. It was a little of everything, just like life."

This answer sticks with us to this day, because our lives turned out to be one battle after another. We had to learn how to fight and keep on fighting, how to win, how to rejoice and be thankful —and then how to do it all over again.

—Danny and Darci Cahill

Introduction

D o you ever look around you and notice those people who seem to always have it all together? They look good and never stop smiling. They coach their kid's team and are involved in something important in the community. It seems like they really know what life is all about, and that's why their lives are great. Their marriage is great. Their kids are great. They love their jobs. They drive the best cars and live in a nice home. They are the All-American family: happy and successful.

We don't believe that for one second!

We believe that no person on this earth is without problems. We all have challenges, difficulties, traumas, tragedies, and those "ugly, secret issues" we are too proud to admit. These are the things we do but don't want to do; the things that are bad for us and ultimately bad for everyone around us, but we always seem to be faced with the temptation to do them, and we just can't help ourselves!

If we get real, of course, we can't blame anyone but ourselves, because we chose to do these things. That's the reality we had to face in order to get out of the cesspool we had made of our lives (we're putting this diplomatically)! We had blamed each other—and everyone and everything except ourselves—for so long, it was a relief just to "come clean," to say, "Okay. I did it. It was my decision." In some cases, we had to say, "All right. We get it. We did that. We take responsibility." Somehow we knew this was the only way we could live the lives we had dreamed of living and make a positive, instead of a negative, impact on the world around us.

There was no real change for the better, however, until we had this epiphany about putting our lives in God's hands. We had tried everything else and failed. Frankly, we had nowhere else to go but "up"! Then, with God's help (He was kind of our referee), we got up from that horrible place, and everything about us seemed different. Every time we looked at each other, we had these goofy smiles on our faces and love in our eyes. Wow! It was such a miracle just to be able to talk to each other again. For months and then years, we actually had hope that our future together would be a good one.

Then, slowly but surely, our lives went upside down again. In some ways it seemed worse than before because we thought we had found the key to happiness and success when we gave ourselves to God. Yet here we were again, in a big mess and not liking each other too much. We continued to do everything we believed we were supposed to do, and still we were miserable.

Frankly, we had to grow up—again. We were in a mess purely because it was time to face some more of our problems—problems we had kept from each other and even from God. And we had to admit that there was a difference this time. We had seen what God had done for us before and knew He could do it again. We knew we needed help from someone who knew us better than we knew ourselves, who saw the big picture when all we could see was our pain and what we wanted or thought we needed right now. All He needed was our willingness and cooperation.

Our journey through one battle of life after another is what this book is about: This is our story of finding God and losing ourselves in His amazing grace—again and again. This is the only way we can face our issues, work through them, and do the great things He wants us to do. We still have issues! But we're working through them, believing that one day they will lose their hold on us. In this context, we really don't mind being the biggest losers ever!

We are living, loving proof that Jesus was right when He said we have to lose our life to find it (or win the game of life). He wasn't telling us we will never enjoy anything we love again. He was telling us that losing our lives means losing the fear, the anger, the rejection, the guilt, the shame, the jealousy, the loneliness, the weakness, the poverty, the utter despair—the addictive, destructive behavior—all the things that make us miserable. That's what we're losing!

And what do we get in return? An extraordinary life! Today we can honestly say that our hearts are filled with God's love, joy, peace, AND the ability to control ourselves (most of the time). Our minds are inundated all the time with fresh and creative ideas. We are beginning to see who we were created to be and what our purpose is; and even when it overwhelms us, we have this amazing "knowing" that God will enable us to be it and do it. Most of all, we know from experience that whether life stabs us in the back or we make our own mess, He is there to give us what we need to get through it.

Right now, our lives are not perfect, but as you read our story, you are going to see how much of the bad stuff we have lost so far, and you are going to see how much greater the gain is. Most of all, you are going to see that we didn't do it by ourselves. In fact, we couldn't have done what we have done alone, and we can't do it today by ourselves. We have lived and continue to live our lives by the love, strength, and wisdom of God and the people He's put in our lives.

Wherever you are spiritually, whatever your situation in life, and whatever your "problems" and "issues" are, please read on. If nothing else, you will enjoy the ride! Our story is as real, honest, and soul-bearing as we can possibly tell it. We are so transparent that some of what you read may shock you. You may relate to it. Or maybe you are living it right now. But one thing is certain: You too can have an extraordinary life by Losing Big.

Dreams Implode

Did you know that one little lie can destroy a whole family? Just one false concept can get someone completely off-track from what they were created to be and to do, causing them and their entire family severe problems. It's usually a very simple thought or idea, but it has an extremely devastating and far-reaching effect: It is a dream killer.

Our life together was nearly ruined by such a deception.

The Lie

In Danny's family, the man of the family had to have an eight-to-five job like all the other men. That kind of profession was the foundation for being a great husband and a great dad. Danny can't tell you that one day his dad sat him down and told him this, nor can he tell you that one day his grandfather sat his father down and drilled that into his head; in fact, they probably never used words to convey this lie. But he can tell you this: They all knew it. It was in the air they breathed. It was like someone or something whispered the lie in their ears and they thought it was their idea. Then they looked around and everything they saw and heard confirmed it. So they believed it was the truth.

Through the years, Danny and his father and perhaps his grandfather all had this idea of what a good husband and father should look like. Unfortunately, none of them really fit that mold, which led to trouble. They weren't just unhappy campers on planet earth. They often made all the people around them, especially their families, unhappy campers too.

Danny has a pretty good idea that his grandfather wasn't doing what he wanted to do in life because of what his father went through growing up. His Grandpa Charlie was a severe alcoholic. Maybe this also had to do with the fact that he was a veteran of World War II, and he probably saw a lot of terrible things.

After the war, Grandpa Charlie was a construction worker and finished concrete. One day he took his brother-in-law, Kenneth, to work with him, and the next thing he knew, he was working for Kenneth's new concrete company. From that point on, Grandpa Charlie resented the fact that Kenneth not only was his boss but also very successful. Grandpa Charlie was simply a sick, angry alcoholic, who saw himself as a victim. In his eyes, he had introduced Kenneth to the concrete business and then built the business for him. He used to say, "If it weren't for me, Kenneth wouldn't have a pot to piss in."

Growing up, Danny felt robbed of a relationship with his grandfather, but alcohol took him away from the entire family. He learned later that his father and Grandma Mary had had the worst of it. Grandpa Charlie would come home drunk and hit Grandma Mary. Then he would chase young Charlie up onto the roof and threaten his life. Life at home was hell for Danny's father, but somehow he managed to rise above it.

Young Charlie decided early on that his terrible home life would not drive him to ruin but would inspire him to greatness. He was very athletic, so he eventually became co-captain and was always a starter on his high school football team. He played baseball and was a champion wrestler, and he was class president for his entire high school career. Obviously, Charlie was well liked and respected by his classmates. Instead of complaining about his home life and using it as an excuse for bad behavior and failure, he fought back and won. Because of this, Danny always saw his father as a hero.

Charlie met his future wife, Sandy, in the seventh grade, and so they were together from the time they were twelve years old. Theirs is a great love story, but it definitely had its challenges. Charlie had received an appointment to the Naval Academy in Annapolis, Maryland, with a wrestling scholarship. The couple's future looked so bright, and Charlie was excited to move away and begin a new life with Sandy, different from the life he knew growing up. That all changed in his senior year, when he and Sandy got pregnant.

Uncle Kenneth urged Charlie not to take the appointment. After all, he had a family on the way and had responsibilities, and this might be the best thing for him. Kenneth used to say, "No worker is worth a damn until they have a family to support." And guess who Charlie went to work for? Uncle Kenneth.

So Charlie gave up his dreams to support his family and be the perfect husband and father. At his father's funeral, a good friend of Charlie's told Danny that his Uncle Kenneth paid his dad less than the other workers on the paving crew, all the while promising to send him to college—a promise he never kept. This surprised Danny because his father had always been great friends with Danny's Uncle Kenneth and looked up to him over the years. In fact, his mother recently told him that Charlie never told her this. They never knew because his father had chosen to forgive Uncle Kenneth, which is a testament to his character.

There is usually an event or belief at the core of a lie that is handed down from generation to generation. Yes, Danny knows Uncle Kenneth was instrumental in establishing the lie in his family, but the men all made the decision to believe that you can't follow your dreams and support a family at the same time. You must sacrifice what you love to do for the people you love.

Early Years

Danny's dad gave up his appointment at the Naval Academy to stay home. He went to work for Uncle Kenneth and gave up his dreams to take care of his new wife and baby. That baby was Danny's oldest sister Cathy. Then a few years later came sister Charla, and three years after that, Danny arrived on August 13, 1969, in Midwest City, Oklahoma. From the beginning, Danny was a force to be reckoned with!

As a youngster, his first best friend was Brian. When they played together, crazy things would happen. For example, when Danny's parents had bought a new dryer, which was a real stretch for them financially, Danny and Brian took Danny's Tonka Trucks and filled them with sand, drove them into the laundry room, and proceeded to fill the new dryer with sand!

Both Brian and Danny's families attended St. Christopher's Episcopal Church in Midwest City, and Brian's parents were Danny's godparents. He and Brian grew apart after Danny's parents moved to another house in Midwest City, but the boys ended up at the same high school later. Still, they weren't as close. Later in life, Danny was shocked to find out that Brian committed suicide, a devastating loss to his family and friends. It felt strange to have once been so close to someone who took his own life, someone who could not find one reason to continue living. Even in his darkest moments and the few times he thought about suicide, there was always someone or something in Danny's life that gave him a glimmer of hope that things could get better. He found out there were lots of people who wanted to help him and could help him—if he would only let them.

To say that Danny was headstrong from the git-go is an understatement. Danny's kindergarten teacher would never forget him. Mrs. Harrell once told his mother that after over forty years of teaching, Danny was the first student who made her consider retirement. The family laughed about this, but Danny was also a pretty sensitive little guy, and although he would laugh too, it made him feel like something was wrong with him.

Danny's mother would also say things like, "If I'd had Danny first, he'd be an only child." Danny translated that into, *I must be really bad.* Of course, if he had asked his mother if she thought he was bad, she would have probably said something like, "I didn't mean you were bad. You are so wonderful! You just happen to be one of the busiest kids I've ever known. I have to work hard to keep up with you! If I'd had you first, I might have decided that taking care of you was all I could handle."

Mrs. Harrell was an awesome teacher, especially for such an "outgoing" student like Danny. He wanted to be in charge and the center of attention. He entered Sooner Rose Elementary in Midwest City, Oklahoma, with a cry to conquer—and it was hard to keep him quiet. This was hard on those who had to teach him that he wasn't the center of the universe, that other people lived here too. On the positive side, it was also the drive that God put in him to keep going no matter what the odds.

Danny looks back on this time as a season of his life when he wasn't afraid. He would speak up when the teacher asked a question. Whatever needed to be done, he would and could do it. This lack of fear continued to dominate his life through high school. When a group of students in his high school formed a band and needed a bass player, he bought a bass, taught himself to play, and became the bass player. When the football coach thought he was too light at 175 pounds to be a strong tackle, he stepped up his workouts and drive during the games to prove to him that size didn't matter when heart was involved.

When Darci met Danny, she went home and told her mother she had met the man she would marry. Later, when Danny weighed 458 pounds, he asked her why she had said that to her mother. What did she see in him that made her know he was "the one"? Without hesitation she answered, "I knew you could accomplish anything."

This is the kind of drive evil wants to control, because when goodness captures the heart and soul of a person like Danny, evil cannot win. So discouragement and despair began to chip away at that fearlessness and confidence. When Danny went to kindergarten, his mother went to work, so he spent half of his days in school and half in day care. The day care was in a home, and while the care giver meant well, she made a critical error with Danny. He had a severe problem with wetting his pants during the day, as well as wetting the bed at night. One day when Danny wet his pants, she stood him in front of the other kids and pointed it out. They didn't react, because they knew what she was doing was wrong. Then she yelled, "Laugh at him!" Danny was devastated as he watched the kids force themselves to laugh. She was trying to motivate him to stop, but instead, she humiliated him. Inside he didn't feel like he had made a mistake; he felt like he was a mistake.

The summer after his kindergarten year, Danny's family and another family took a trip to the Royal Gorge in Colorado. Danny turned six on that vacation, and remembers singing at the top of his voice, "Shoo fly, don't bother me, shoo fly, don't bother me, shoo fly, don't bother me, 'cause I belong to somebody!" They explored caves and found fool's gold, stayed in cabins, and saw hummingbirds.

At the Royal Gorge, Danny leaned over the railing and his mother screamed at him, ran up to grab him, and then got very angry with him. Of course, she was afraid he would drop over the railing, but her reaction seemed to go right through Danny. After that, he began to overreact whenever he became afraid. He would automatically begin yelling and screaming if anything scared him. Panic became his co-pilot.

Still, overall it was an incredible trip. The thing that stuck out the most, however, was that his older sister carved into a piece of old wood, "I Cathy say Danny is 6 today! Almont, Colorado." She gave it to him as a birthday gift, and it meant more to him than any other gift that year. Later in life, when he tried to find it, he couldn't. To this day, he doesn't know where it is and would love to have it back.

Cathy has always been very special to Danny. When his mother went back to work, his twelve-year-old sister became his mother. Cathy raised him. She punished him when he did wrong. She gave him his first penny and taught him to read. When he was in kindergarten, he could read at a sixth-grade level. People were amazed, but it was because Cathy was teaching him to read what she was reading! Obviously, Danny was very bright to understand so much so quickly, but Cathy was the one who taught him.

There was a down side to this arrangement. They developed a "mother-son" relationship that worked well when they were younger and it was necessary. When Danny became a young adult, however, this caused some conflicts and tension between them. Nevertheless, Danny continues to love his sister and to this day appreciates all she did for him.

Danny's hero was his father, Charlie. Because Charlie had played football, baseball, and wrestled in high school—and Danny wanted to be like his hero—he started wrestling at the YMCA when he was five years old. He also began playing football with the Purple Vikings in Midwest City/Del City. His father was the assistant coach, and that was fine with Danny. He looked up to him, and the stories he heard about him were awesome.

Danny was told that his dad had only been in three fights in his life. All three were about his mother, and in all three his opponent hit the ground after one punch from Charlie. Danny thought he was the strongest man in the world. Sometimes that strength scared him, though. One day his dad got so angry that he punched holes in his sister's bedroom door. Although this was frightening, the family was never afraid Charlie would hit any of them. They knew he wasn't like that.

Unfortunately, Danny compared himself with his dad and never seemed to measure up. He was always trying to live up to the excellence he saw in his father, his mother, and his two older sisters, but he never felt that what he did was good enough. Even though he excelled in many things and scored in the top two percent of most tests, it was rare for him to feel like a success.

One of the reasons for this was that Danny would "coast." Things came so easily to him that he would only study just enough to get an A. He would only work hard enough to make the team, stay on the team, and then do his best to help win the game. He knew he was capable of so much more, but he was too lazy to go for it. Getting by was a recurring theme in his life. He watched how hard his parents and his sisters worked—Cathy actually was valedictorian of her class—but he felt like a failure.

Although Danny loves sports, he has one character trait that has made it difficult for him to participate, particularly in one-on-one sports like wrestling: He hates to see the other person lose! For that reason, wrestling was definitely not his passion. He always had butterflies in his stomach before a match, and he hated going one-on-one with someone. He just couldn't get past the fact that one of them was going to win and the other one would lose. Even when he won, he didn't really feel like a winner.

Being on a football team was different, however. The Purple Vikings was an important part of Danny's early life, from five to ten years old. His team not only won games, but also dominated their league. He felt like a winner on that team, as well as an important member. He was tough, and his nickname was "Bone-crusher Cahill." Just that name made him believe he could hit harder than anyone else.

Danny's head coach was a genius at getting the boys to play well, but there were times when his tactics seemed very wrong to Danny. For example, there was a player who needed to be tougher on the field, so the coach put Danny across from him at practice. Over and over again, Danny had to "kill" this boy while the coach screamed, "You get through Cahill or else!" The boy never could, and the coach sent him home early.

After practice, Danny felt like a bully instead of a hero. Even though he felt tough, he also felt dirty, like he had done something wrong and was rewarded for it. It had always been hard for him to win at another's expense, and this was his worst nightmare. He also felt used in a very bad way, as if the coach had used his gift and drive to break another kid. That day at football practice was etched in his mind forever. He swore he would never do that again.

Danny always wanted to be good, so guilt was a huge part of his life! He had a guilty conscience about everything he thought he had done wrong. He had actually bullied the boy next door for a semester because he was jealous of him. He always felt guilty, and recently he was glad to be able to apologize to the man on Facebook! Even if Danny received a gift, he would feel guilty. He would think, *I've got enough already and shouldn't have gotten it.* If someone had a need and Danny didn't meet it—even if someone else was better able to meet the need and did—he would feel guilty.

He didn't feel guilty about winning football games with his team, however! The Purple Vikings went to bowl games in other states, and they felt like a pro football team. They always won their league championship and went undefeated most of the time. One year, they had played all their games without having one point scored on them. Then, with a few minutes to go in a game near the end of the season, the coach decided to leave in their second string players after a turnover on the five-yard line. As a result, the opposing team scored a touchdown, which destroyed the Purple Vikings hope of having a perfect season.

Although they went on to win the league championship, Danny and his teammates felt like that one game was a loss because their perfect record had been broken. Then one player, Norman Brodeur, spoke up and said, "You did the right thing, Coach. Everyone's gotta play." Danny never forgot those wise words from his friend and teammate.

In Danny's eyes, his father was the best in everything he did. He didn't see Charlie's failures or the times he got discouraged and almost quit. Therefore, Danny grew up expecting himself to be perfect in everything he did. He had a winning state of mind,

15

and anything less than the best wasn't good enough. This mindset set him up for failure and humiliation again and again. He would always fall just a little short of what he believed was the best. He would accomplish so much but never feel like the hero he was desperate to be.

One day he would have to come to grips with what it took to be that hero.

School Days

Danny continued to make his mark in the first grade, and a choice example happened during tumbling class. All the kids got in line to do the crab crawl, and he passed everyone. He wasn't supposed to get out of line, but he disobeyed in order to pass the other kids. He wanted everyone to see that he could crab crawl so good! It meant a lot to him for people to see what he could do, and that same performance attitude would serve him well when he took off his shirt and bared both his soul and his 430-pound body to 20 million viewers on television. There is nothing Danny likes better than a challenge!

Danny was good on the rings at six years old, and an older student named Gary Beach stopped him in the hall at school and said, "Let me see that muscle! Oh my gosh! You are so strong!" That meant the world to Danny. He hungered for a pat on the back. His father was very quiet, perhaps because of his troubled past, and rarely vocalized his approval. However, it did not dawn on Danny that there were many kids in his school who never got any pats on the back, nor did he realize that he was excelling in some things and being noticed for them. Like most kids, he could not see his own achievements from a realistic perspective, and so the insatiable hunger to be recognized grew.

On the positive side, Danny was developing a champion attitude and credits his mother's mother, Grandma Ada Walker, for much of this. She spent time with each of her grandkids and encouraged them. She never put them down. She would say, "Ohhhhh Danny. You are so good at that! You can do anything! And so good-lookin' too!" She made each one of them believe they were amazing human beings. She was always an optimist, and she was crazy fun. Danny's friends still talk about her to this day.

Danny will say, "If there was one person who built me up as a kid, it was Ada." When he won *The Biggest Loser*, his sister held up a picture of Grandma Ada. On the back it said, "There'll be no more tears in Heaven." Danny had sung that song at Ada's funeral. She was the first person close to him who had died, and she meant the world to him. He wishes she had lived to see all he has accomplished today.

Danny never knew Grandma Ada's husband, Grandfather Monroe. Danny's mother and Grandma Ada used to say that Danny resembled him. They were both colorblind and flat-footed! Not the best qualities to bind you with a grandfather, but it made Danny feel close to him even though they had never met.

Danny's mother Sandy was fifteen when she lost her father, who was only forty-seven. Because his mother had lost her father at such an early age, Danny developed a fear that he would lose his parents when he was young. He was certain they would die before he finished high school. Just the thought terrified him for years.

After first grade, something very upsetting happened to Danny. His sister Charla wanted to go to another school which meant the other siblings would have to transfer as well. It was in the same school district, so they would end up at the same high school, but it would take Danny away from all of his friends and the elementary school he loved. He put up a fight, but he lost and was forced to make the change.

For a long time, Danny felt like an outsider at the new school. He had to make new friends, and that was hard for him back then. He also wanted a girlfriend. One day he noticed a little blonde-headed girl in the school play and thought to himself, *She's gonna be my girlfriend!* There was a boy in the play with her, and Danny just knew he was his rival. He thought, *I'm gonna take her away from him, even if I have to beat him up!* Usually boys his age shunned girls, but Danny began to chase them. From that point on, he always had to have a girlfriend. It made him feel good about himself, like he fit in with the rest of the kids.

Despite his rocky beginning at the new school, by the third grade Danny was chosen for an advanced class called "Seekers." These children were chosen because they liked to learn. The class met before school, and it gave Danny a sense of being special and a part of something important. He felt he was smart and could do anything! This helped to define him in a positive way, but it was also during this time that he began to struggle with his weight.

Before a growth spurt, boys will generally gain weight. They go out before going up. This is normal. But Danny's weight gain was above normal. Either he was compensating for changing schools, or (most likely) the problem had been waiting to emerge for some time. He began to gain weight between his second and third grade years, and he kept gaining until he was overweight by the end of third grade.

During the rest of elementary school, Danny played football and was still very popular. The way he dealt with this obvious "failure" of being overweight was to become the class clown. He had several girlfriends but also was hurt a couple of times. During a dance, he heard a girl say, "I don't want to dance with Danny. I already took a shower this morning." People laughed, and he was mortified. Nevertheless, he continued to be the life of the party and was voted "most humorous" several times. On the outside he was funny and had lots of friends, but on the inside he often was depressed, unhappy, and felt alone.

Danny's sixth-grade teacher, Suzanne Phelps-Wylie, was one person who made him feel handsome. Every morning he would walk in and she would have to have her "Danny hug." She made him look forward to school and gave him a sense of worth he desperately needed. He would look at his overweight body in the mirror and ask, "Am I worth it?" When he looked at Mrs. Phelps-Wylie, he forgot the other kids' laughter and her smile gave him the answer: "Danny, I wouldn't change a thing about you. You are perfect just the way you are."

Growing Up

Junior high school was a shock. Socially, Danny matured a little slower than his peers, and his parents had thought about holding him back in the sixth grade, but his teacher talked them out of it. He made good grades, and she told them he would catch up maturity-wise. He went from being a big fish (literally) in a little pond with only certain kids poking fun at him, to having the entire school making fun of him. At least, that's the way it seemed to him. He felt awkward and reacted by spending more time at home in his room, messing around on his computer.

The seventh grade was especially tough, but not as tough as eighth grade. His football team lost all their games and went "defeated." If that wasn't bad enough, for the first time he sat on the bench the entire season. His father asked the coach, "What's wrong? Danny has always been at the top of his class in sports! Why in the world is he not starting?"

The coach answered, "He's more interested in goofing off than playing football." And what he said was true. Danny was always getting into mischief, like taking pieces of grass, "tickling" the ear of someone's helmet to make them think it was a bug, and causing them to freak out. He tied players' shoelaces together, and when the coach called for them, they all jumped up and fell flat on their faces. More than ever, Danny compensated for all his insecurities about his weight by being funny.

At this point, none of the girls he was interested in were interested in him. He felt that his life was in shambles and contemplated going to the First National Bank in Oklahoma City, where his Grandma Mary worked, and jumping off the top. He craved attention, but the kind he was getting was not what he wanted!

When summer arrived, Danny resented that he had to work with his father, who now had his own business. Just before Danny was born, Charlie had left Uncle Kenneth's concrete business when they had a disagreement. Charlie was a salaried employee and had worked twelve- to fourteen-hour days the entire week when Kenneth told him he had to work on Saturday. Charlie said, "No way! I'm going home to spend some time with my family."

Kenneth replied, "Then don't come back."

The following Monday, Charlie went to work at a surveying company for a very small salary. He also went to school, and in 1969 he got his land surveyor's license. In 1978, he started Cahill Land Surveying. He expected all of his children to help in the business, so at nine years old, Danny was holding the chain and the pole for his dad when he wasn't in school. His sisters didn't like this any more than Danny did, especially Charla. She was a real "girly girl." One day, she wore perfume to work and a swarm of bees attacked her. It was terrifying and so after that, Charlie let her stay home to answer the phone. Cathy and Danny were often angry that she got off so easy.

At thirteen, Danny knew a lot more about land surveying and was performing more important tasks. Charlie gave him a big raise, so now he was making $3.50 an hour! That was huge to Danny, not only because of having more money in his pocket, but also because his father had shown his approval, which was rare in those days. Danny and his father also fished a lot. They got up early in the morning and ran out to the pond in Uncle Kenneth's sand pit. There, they put the catch from the night before in a trash can, set and bait the trot line again, and went to work. They would come back during lunch and also at five after work, each time putting any fish they had caught in the trashcan and baiting the trotline.

Although Danny mostly hated having to work when all the other kids were going to the pool and having fun, he always had spending money and enjoyed working with his father. They became close friends during those years, and his father taught him the value of work and the rewards of working hard.

When Danny wasn't working and fishing with his dad, he was on his computer. Sometimes he would stay up all night on the Bulletin Board System, which was like the Internet before it was the Internet. He would also hack into other computers like some of his friends. One of his computer buddies actually went to prison for hacking and was then recruited by the FBI to stop other hackers. Danny also did a lot of gaming, which was a lot less risky!

In the ninth grade, Danny lost a little weight and a few girls were interested in him. He went to the Sweetheart Dance with a girl named Audra. She was very pretty and smart, and they were in the same homeroom. After the dance, he ignored her. Now he realizes that maybe he wanted to hurt someone the way others had been hurting him, but he regrets his actions to this day.

The time for high school came and Danny was really excited, but he was about to have one of the worst years of his life. He had gained back the weight he had lost in the ninth grade. No girl was interested in him. Although he started on the junior varsity football team as a sophomore, he was terribly self-conscious and felt out-of-place. Even his comedy routine was becoming dry.

He made some new friends who were into strange things, such as making homemade bombs and booby-traps, and his memories of that time are very dark. These guys got into the Goth movement, changed their names, and began doing drugs like LSD. Danny felt like he was losing himself, so he stopped hanging out with them.

After his sophomore year, he decided to change. This is always the key with Danny: commitment. Once he makes that quality decision, a decision that comes from deep inside and refuses to quit "no matter what," then things start to happen. That summer he worked with his father and began running until he was doing three miles a day. He ate very little and drank a lot of diet soda to keep from feeling too hungry. By the time his junior year in high school started, he had lost 75 pounds, and he continued to lose weight. When he went back to school, people didn't recognize him. The girls seemed to be whispering to themselves about him, and that made Danny feel great for a change.

He went to his first rock concert, and while the group sang their biggest hit, the lead singer wore the hat Danny had thrown onto the stage! He saw the love and admiration the crowd had for the band and craved it. He thought, *I want to play music!* That was when he learned that a band in school needed a bass player, so he bought a bass guitar at a pawn shop, taught himself to play, and began playing with that band. They performed at a school dance, and Danny got his first real girlfriend. Life was looking up!

Music became Danny's new obsession. He stayed up all night playing and learning songs. He began writing songs inspired by his girlfriends, parties, friends, and life in general. In his words, he was "hitting on all cylinders!" By the time he graduated from high school, he was a very popular guy and threw the senior party. Everyone knew him, and most people liked him.

He wrote in several yearbooks, "Look for me on MTV!"

They ended up seeing him on *The Biggest Loser* at 430 pounds.

The Transition Begins

How do you go from being the most popular guy in high school to "*The Biggest Loser*"? It's not easy!

Danny went to college and began as a computer science/ engineering major. He did this because he liked fishing, computers, and music; and computers were the only "real" way a man could make a good living out of that list. After two years, however, he decided it was stupid to follow his skills alone. He needed to follow his passion. He didn't want to do something he was good at but didn't have a heart to do. Although his father had quit his job with Uncle Kenneth and done something he wanted to do, he was dismayed when Danny changed his major to music.

Danny loved studying the music business and songwriting, while he continued to write songs and do a lot of performing. His teachers recognized his ability and gave him a fee waiver scholarship the last year at school. He graduated from Rose State College with an Associate in the Arts degree and a Contemporary Music Certificate. For a time, he got a job playing with a band called PC Quest. They made it to Billboard's Top 40, and Danny was having the time of his life until the band signed with RCA Records and left him behind. This was an experience he had had too often. Several of the bands he had been a part of through the years had nearly made it and then fallen apart. He had believed PC Quest was going to be his big break, so this was a terrible blow to him.

When PC Quest moved on without him, Danny was living with his parents and working with his father part time. He began working full time with his dad, but he became so depressed that he began staying in his room when he was not working. He didn't want to hear or think about music.

One day his father came into his bedroom to talk to him. Charlie had come out of his shell and had become a "cowboy poet." He often read his poetry at various venues, and Danny and his family were amazed at the depth of understanding he revealed in his writing. He told Danny that auditions were being held for a big Fourth of July show in downtown Oklahoma City, and he was going to go down and read one of his poems. He asked Danny to go with him and try out. Danny fought him until he saw how much it meant to his dad, then he did it only as a favor.

The day of the audition, Danny sat on the curb outside the studio, playing his guitar and waiting to be called. Two pretty girls walked up to him and began competing for his attention. One was a Korean girl named Hui Cha, and the other became his wife—ironically she would be the reason he would give up his music again.

Dreams implode within us because we are deceived into thinking they are either impossible to achieve or we are not capable of achieving them. Danny's love for Darci would bring him back under the lie that he could not be a good husband and pursue the thing he loved to do. He would again believe that it was impossible for him to make a good living and support a family by pursuing a career in the music business.

However, God would use Darci's love for Danny to turn everything around—in both their lives.

A Free Spirit

We all know someone whom we adore and stand in awe of one minute and are completely shocked and repulsed by what they say and do the next minute. Sometimes that someone is ourself! These are the free spirits, who will either transform the world around them into something incredibly lovely and alive or destroy it with seemingly little thought or remorse. They can build an empire or leave a wake of grief behind them. So what makes them go one way or the other?

We believe that when "lights" like these enter the world, darkness immediately goes to work to extinguish them. Yes, all of us have to come to grips with our weaknesses, faults, and failings, but this seems particularly difficult for those who are extremely gifted and charismatic. In fact, the only way a free spirit can truly defeat the darkness that seeks to destroy them is to latch on to someone who is not only greater than the darkness, but also greater than their own self-deceit and willfulness.

For someone that smart, that talented, and that capable—only God will do. However, as long as they go it alone, God help us all!

Tomboy...Not Entirely

Darci Ann McBride was her parents' unexpected delight. Quint and Beverly McBride already had two children; Dacri and Dan were fifteen months apart and good playmates. They thought their family was complete, but God thought differently. Darci arrived on the scene several years later on August 20, 1970, at Baptist Hospital in Oklahoma City. Her perfect, round head and big, brown eyes were Beverly's joy.

Shortly afterward, when Darci was six-months-old, the family moved to Omaha, Nebraska, where Darci's father owned and operated a Yamaha motorcycle dealership. She and her older siblings were raised on motorbikes. In fact, Darci learned to ride a motorbike before she could ride a bicycle! Her first was a bright yellow Honda she named "Sunshine."

When Darci was four years old, the family moved back to Edmond, Oklahoma, because her father's father, Grandpa Bruce, had started a new business and wanted Darci's father to help him. Grandpa Bruce was a colorful character. He left home at thirteen to become a rodeo rider and had done well for a country boy, owning and operating both a 360-acre farm and his heat and air business. On top of supporting the family, he also took care of horses, cows, pigs, chickens, hound dogs, and a crop field.

Grandma Deanie, whom everyone called "Sweetheart," was an amazing cook, and there was nothing like walking back to the farmhouse, smelling what was cooking in her kitchen. Sweetheart was Darci's favorite person to be with because she gave Darci her full love and attention. Darci was glad to be living closer to them. Her earliest and best memories were of spending time on their farm outside of Stillwater, Oklahoma. She loved being outdoors, exploring the land, and playing with the dogs and cats and other animals. Being in the country was magical to her, and she often preferred staying with her grandparents on the farm rather than going on family vacations. Darci's free spirit flourished on the farm. Her summers were filled with bareback riding a quarter horse named Missy, crawdad fishing in the creek, and bathing the baby pigs in her grandparent's bathtub. While she loved this, it often made a mess for Sweetheart to clean!

In Edmond, Darci's family was a typical, middle-class, American family. They lived in a three-bedroom, two-bath house, with a big backyard. They had two collies and a cat, and animals were always in Darci's perfect picture. Their family life was good, but from an early age, Darci felt different. She was four and a half years younger than her brother Dan and six years younger than her sister Dacri. Being so much younger than her siblings, she felt like an only child and spent a lot of time by herself. As a result, her imagination became her playmate.

Darci's dolls played roles in the worlds she created. She would make up plays and commercials and often act them out in front of her bathroom mirror. One day Dacri saw her pretending and asked, "Who are you talking to?" Without waiting for an answer, Dacri shook her head and said, "You are so weird." Of course, she was probably amused at her little sister's antics, but over time and after hearing this kind of thing often, Darci's impression that she was different became her belief—and not a positive one.

Like Danny's family, there was lots of love and many happy memories in Darci's family. Holidays and special occasions were always celebrated with great preparation and excitement, and family time was always made an event. Darci's oldest memory comes from when she was three years old, and her dad surprised the family by taking them to Disneyland in California. Although she was only three, she remembers holding her father's hand while watching the parade and fireworks.

The McBride's were a very theatrical family. Darci's dad spent time in his youth singing on the local radio show in Stillwater, Oklahoma, and her mother was on the modern dance team at a girl's college in Missouri. Perhaps because of this, Dacri, Dan, and Darci would make up plays and sing songs for the family. Almost every weekend, their family would spend time with other families. There was always good food, lots of laughter, and love.

Darci's parents were very sociable, and people were naturally drawn to them. Her father was the kind of man that people love to be around; full of intelligence and very charismatic. He always went out of his way to help others. Her mother was a kind-hearted and thoughtful listener, always choosing to see the best in people. These were qualities Darci inherited from them. As a little girl, she was also very sensitive spiritually, another reason she felt different. She loved God and felt that He was with her all the time. But when she was about seven years old, she began to sense a different presence. It was dark, evil, and frightening. There were times at night when she felt like something loathsome was breathing down her neck. She would run to her mother in her parents' room, her body shaking, and she would cry hysterically, "He's after me! He's after me!"

Darci's mother would sit up on the bed and take her in her arms. "Who's after you?"

"The devil!"

Her mother would look at her intently. "You belong to Jesus, don't you?"

"Yes."

"He's in your heart, so the devil can't get you." Then Beverly would put Darci in the bed, between her and Darci's father. Beverly would wonder at how this happy, bright, and seemingly fearless child could become so terrified. It had to be something spiritual.

Darci immediately relaxed in her parents' arms. Her daddy would protect her. Her mother knew Jesus better than anyone, and Jesus beat the devil! This occurred several times in the course of a year before it stopped altogether, but the darkness was not finished with her yet.

When Darci was eight, her parents sold their house and began building a home on a two-and-a-half-acre lot in Edmond, Oklahoma. Her father had originally calculated that it would take five to six months to complete, but it took five years! During that time, they lived in a small camper trailer on an acreage just outside of Edmond. Looking back, Darci sees how odd it was for her family to live in a trailer so small they could pull it behind a pickup truck. They made the best of living in a small space and each had chores to do. Through this Darci learned from her mother that whether you live in a camper or a mansion, whether you are poor or rich, you should always take care of what you have to the best of your ability, including yourself.

Her siblings were teenagers and weren't very happy about the situation, but to Darci it was just another adventure in the great outdoors. While Dacri was embarrassed to be picked up by her prom date at the camper, Darci was having the time of her life exploring the creeks and woods. She raised rabbits, squirrels, and loved her favorite raccoon named Sophie. For one so young, she made the best of whatever situation she was in, even the cold showers.

As it turned out, they would live in the camper for five years and only get to live in the house her parents built for a little over three years. Despite the inconvenience and difficulty of living in the camper, Darci's mother kept a smile on her face and made the situation as pleasant as possible. It was easy for Darci to dismiss the times she sensed tension between her parents, but moving around like this made her feel like a nomad. When she met Danny, she envied him, growing up in one place he could call home and to which he could always return. However, she would not trade the fun she had living in the country!

Darci always had friends. While her family lived in the camper, her best friend was Amber, who lived in a large house on another acreage in the same neighborhood. They became quick partners in crime, as both were little tomboys who rode motorbikes, built forts, and played with pocketknives. Darci still played with dolls and brought her Barbies to the creek to play! She was a happy, carefree kid.

The gift of singing emerged when Darci was very young. Grandma Deanie recalled hearing Darci singing in the garden on their farm when she was four years old, and she and Grandpa Bruce were both impressed with her ability to carry a tune perfectly. Although her mother often bribed her with money to get her to sing for family and friends, secretly Darci loved to perform.

In sixth grade, Darci performed her first solo at a contest and got the highest award. It was the first time she felt she was great at something, and it was something she loved to do! She had an awesome music teacher who encouraged her, Mr. Orvis, and she developed a passion for singing and music that has never left.

Mr. Orvis had Darci perform a Christmas duet with a girl named Kathy. They sang, "Dear Santa, We Just Got the Measles," and discovered a mutual love for music. Darci's friends have been extremely important to her, and through the years she has had many great friendships, but Kathy would be a life-long friend, through thick and thin. From the moment they met through today, they have talked almost every day. Moreover, Kathy would play a significant role in Darci's life when they got older.

When Darci was in third grade the family began going to church, and she loved it. It was a Charismatic congregation, with contemporary Christian music and a pastor who was a well-known and respected preacher and teacher of the Bible. When she was young, Darci walked to the altar to "get saved" nearly every service. Like many kids growing up in church, she thought anything she did during the week that was bad disqualified her for Heaven; so she "walked the aisle" many Sundays! She also sensed there was something these Christians had that she wanted and still didn't have.

Darci spent her summers at church camps and when she was old enough became a part of the youth group. She felt the love of God but never seemed to be able to really know Him. This was another confirmation to her that she was different from all the other kids in a negative way. Instead of voicing her fears to her family, youth pastor, or Christian friends, she buried them by continuing to stay busy in church activities. Then disaster struck.

Their pastor got into big trouble, the church was in shock, and her family gradually stopped going to church. Darci was in middle school, and by that time she and her older brother and sister were extremely involved in so many school activities that it seemed like a good time to cut something out of their lives. Her brother was a champion wrestler, her sister travelled internationally and performed with the swing choir, Darci was singing in various activities in school, and her family tried to attend each event in which their children were involved. Furthermore, by quietly walking away from church, they could simply forget the pain of the situation. It was almost like it never happened. Darci learned early on that denial and escape were great ways of dealing with conflict.

Pompon Girl

When Darci entered her freshman year in high school, she wanted to try out for cheerleader, but she was a little overweight. Her father had been a state champion wrestler, and so was her brother Dan, so her dad had her do the only thing he knew to do, which was "pull weight" like a wrestler who was getting ready for a match. This regimen had worked for him and then her brother Dan.

Unfortunately, her dad's approach to weight loss was extreme. He put Darci on a severe diet and made her do daily, hard-core workouts and weekly weigh-ins. If she didn't lose the number of pounds he thought she should have lost, he wouldn't let her eat that day. She hated it at the time, but now she is grateful for a father who cared enough to give her the tough love she needed. She also credits his training for leading to many other great experiences and opportunities.

Not only did she make the pompon squad, but by her senior year, Darci was number four in the nation individually. Her squad was number one in the nation. In college, she went on to work for the National Cheerleading Association (NCA), the first and only cheerleading organization in America at the time. In her sophomore year, she became the youngest head instructor for the NCA. At nineteen years old, she was running cheerleading camps with hundreds of girls participating, dozens of adult sponsors, and several staff members serving beneath her.

Another great payoff for all Darci's hard work was a great figure and lots of energy for being on the pompon squad, singing in the choir, and dancing. Her father's training and all these activities made her high school years a fantastic time and gave her great confidence. Her parents were always there, supporting her as they had her brother and sister.

In the summer after her freshman year, the McBrides finally moved into their new home. All Darci's friends wanted to hang out at her house, and not just because it was new and had lots of room. Everyone loved her parents, and the McBrides liked nothing more than having lots of people around.

Darci also had discovered how much she loved performing. Whether singing and dancing or leading a cheer, she shone in the limelight—at least on the outside. Although she felt wonderful while performing, there was a downside. She felt like the ugly girl who could only be accepted by her talent, abilities, and hard work. She didn't see how beautiful she was.

This lie probably took hold when Darci's father made a stupid rule. He required her to wear makeup to summer pompon workouts. She didn't think it was fair, because she had to be there at 5:30 a.m., and by the end of the workout the makeup was dripping off her sweaty face. When she asked him why, he told her, "You just aren't pretty enough to go without wearing makeup." From that moment, she was deeply insecure about her appearance.

Later, when she met Danny, her sister confirmed Darci's belief that she was unattractive when she asked, "How did you ever get a guy that good looking?" While her sister probably meant she thought Danny was handsome, which was a compliment to Darci,

Darci took the comment to mean something quite different. From her way of looking at things, she was only popular and got dates because of her personality and talents, and maybe her cute figure. Boys could not like her because of her looks. She was not pretty. She had to work hard to convince them she was at least attractive.

Party Girl

After graduating from high school, Darci was accepted to the University of Oklahoma in Norman, Oklahoma. She went from being a big fish in a little pond to being a little fish in a big pond, and her wonderful life turned into a constant struggle. She pledged a sorority but immediately felt inferior to all the beautiful girls. She also had a hard time with girls who seemed petty and shallow. She wasn't used to not having deep connections with her girlfriends. The old lie of being different haunted her. Was she smart enough, pretty enough, and good enough for them?

Academically, she changed her major every semester and skipped a lot of her classes. Except for her work with the NCA, she ran from her responsibilities. She became increasingly depressed and felt lonely, but she always made time to party with her friends. She began to drink because alcohol made her feel good about herself. It transformed her bleak existence into something exciting, giving her the ability to "freely feel" her emotions—or so she thought.

Darci was also riddled with guilt and shame. Her parents had gotten into serious financial trouble and lost their house, but they were still finding a way to pay for her college education. She hated herself for wasting their money. If that wasn't enough guilt, everything really fell apart in her freshmen year, when she gave up her virginity to someone she thought she loved. After it was over, she walked back to her dorm room feeling as though a core part of her being had been ripped out. She knew she had betrayed herself and given up a precious gift God had given her to give to her future husband. To make matters worse, the man she had slept with was her girlfriend's ex-boyfriend, so she also believed she had betrayed her friend.

Instead of getting help, she compensated by becoming increasingly tough, almost callous. She decided she was "a woman in control," powerful and able to decide on her own what was best for her. Buying into this deception, soon she was drinking heavily and chasing boys, trying to prove she was beautiful and desirable. Inside she was insecure, lonely, and often frightened; outside, her grades were good enough to keep her in her sorority, she managed to do her work with the NCA, and she tried to believe the carefree, in-control image she was showing to the world.

In the middle of her junior year, Darci was fed up with the struggle to keep up appearances and to be worthy of her parents' financial sacrifice, so she quit school. She moved in with her parents, who were now living in a doublewide trailer on her grandparents' farm in Stillwater. Grandpa Bruce had passed away, and her parents were taking care of Grandma Deanie. Her father managed the farm and the rental properties, which was a full-time job, and her mother worked in Oklahoma City. The loss of their home and the bankruptcy had taken its toll on their relationship, and for the first time, Darci knew things weren't quite right between her parents.

Within a few months, Darci's mother decided to leave Stillwater because the commute to Oklahoma City was too much for her to do every day. She rented a house in the city, and Darci decided to move there with her. Soon after that, Darci got a job working for a new sports grill as a waitress. She found she was very good at it, and she liked the money and the energy of the staff and clientele. The bar scene also made it easy to get a drink whenever she wanted one.

So Darci and her mother became unlikely roommates. Her dad would show up on the weekends to spend time with them and pay bills, which took a good share of her mother's paycheck. Thus, Darci would help pay Beverly's way for any extra activities. Her father's behavior seemed more and more erratic, which was another good reason to stay away until the early hours of the morning and sleep late whenever he was there. When he moved into the house with them, he couldn't handle Darci's lifestyle and began trying to control her. Of course, Darci resisted his attempts and would do the opposite of what he commanded her to do. It wasn't long before she moved out.

For a while she lived with her mother's mother, whom she called GG, and who was twice widowed. Darci's grandfather had passed away when her mother was five years old. GG remarried, but her mother's stepfather had died before Darci was born. So Darci never knew either grandfather. Since then, GG had remained single. GG and Darci had always been close because their personalities were so much alike. Like Darci, however, GG was strong, independent, and loved being with people.

Both of Darci's grandmothers were always special to her. They always reminded her of the children's book by Patricia and Richard Scarry, *The Country Mouse and the City Mouse*. The country mouse was Grandma Deanie and the city mouse was GG, and Darci had the best of both worlds in them. She also inherited great character traits from them. She has GG's strength, tenacity, and love for people; and she has Grandma Deanie's compassion, love to serve others, and the ability to enjoy the little things in life.

GG passed away while Danny was on *The Biggest Loser*, but Grandma Deanie is 92 at this writing and going strong. They were the ones who remained Darci's "safe havens." She knew she could always go to them, never had to prove anything to them, and would receive unconditional love even when she was not living right. However, they always told her the truth.

Darci thought she had found the perfect roommate in GG, who loved her "evening cocktails." As misery loves company, in the beginning she and Darci spent many nights drinking and talking into the wee hours of the night. For awhile GG loved having Darci live with her, but after too many times of seeing her stroll in at four in the morning or not come home until noon the next day, she became frustrated with her. It wasn't long before their occasional late-night drinking powwows became opportunities for GG to voice her concern about the way Darci was living her life. She tried to give her the wisdom of age and experience.

Darci rejected GG's advice just as she had her mother and father's, and she decided to move to Tulsa. Dacri and her husband lived there, and they had asked Darci to help them save some money by living with them for one year. Her job would be to take care of their son, who was one year old, while they both worked. However, within weeks of moving in with her sister's family, Darci realized she needed more money to support her lifestyle, so she took a job waiting tables. Then her working hours and the partying that followed conflicted with taking care of her nephew. After three months, her sister and brother-in-law had had enough. Darci moved back in with her mother and father in Oklahoma City and went back to her old job at the sports grill.

Darci knew she was driving her family crazy and that they were extremely disappointed in her. Nevertheless, she continued to come home drunk several nights a week and was very unhappy whenever she sobered up. During this time, her brother Dan was the person she trusted most. He had always been very protective of her through the years, which made him a safe place. There were many nights that she would call him in Atlanta, where he was living. Very drunk and always crying, she would try to explain how lost she felt. He listened to her, but the phone calls only upset him. Feeling desperate because he lived so far away, he called their parents, thinking they could help her. These calls would just fuel Darci's mother's need to keep her close and her father's need to control her. Once he woke her up while she was "sleeping it off" and made her urinate in a cup, so he could have her tested for drugs. The truth was, she had tried a few drugs early on, but had decided alcohol was her drug of choice.

There were times when Darci tried to leave her parents' house. After all, she made enough money to live on her own. However, every time she tried to leave, her mother would cry and beg her to stay.

Later, Darci realized that things were so bad between her parents that they welcomed any kind of diversion from having to face their own problems. Although having Darci in the house was difficult, it took their attention away from their own failing relationship.

After a year of living like this, Darci heard about auditions for the dance team that would support the semi-pro basketball team Oklahoma City had acquired. She pulled herself together, tried out, and was accepted. About the same time, she was hired to be one of the singers at the premiere karaoke bar in Bricktown in Oklahoma City called "O'Brien's Piano and Karaoke Bar—the cool place to be." Singing and dancing gave her a zest for life again.

She dated and had a couple of relationships, but nothing lasted. Ironically, Darci's first major relationship was with a recovering alcoholic, who eventually got tired of her drunken antics. Within a month after they broke up, she entered a relationship with a man who was ten years older. Guess what they had in common? Drinking! They spent their time together getting wasted. Darci thought she was in love, but this relationship only lasted about ten months.

Darci was heartbroken and depressed because the last man had at least made her feel beautiful. True to form, she drowned her sorrows with alcohol. Meanwhile, her college friends were graduating and getting married. They were moving on, and she was stuck in her rut, alone, lonely, and depressed. She continued to drink and party while taking some joy in dancing for the basketball team and singing at the karaoke bar.

Needs

Darci looks back on her childhood and growing-up years and realizes her life was not the picture-perfect world she chose to believe it was for a long time. She now sees that Grandpa Bruce, although being a wonderful man, was not just a colorful character, who lived on an idyllic farm in the country. Although she received his love and adoration, she found out later that he was also a hoarder of his money, extremely paranoid, and had been physically abusive to her dad in his youth. He buried all his money in the yard instead of putting it in banks. Banks, of course, would steal your money! When he passed away, the family had to burn the grass around the house to dig up whatever he had left Grandma Deanie! In spite of these discoveries, Darci still remembers Grandpa Bruce with adoration.

Darci's father inherited these unfortunate tendencies. When her parents lost their house, fear of lack took hold of him and he began to keep everything. By the time she went home to live with them, there were several storage facilities filled with stuff that should have been thrown out or given away. Furthermore, the storage costs helped to eat away what little money her mother brought home. There were other issues that they ignored as Darci grew up, and these later came to a head. Her parents were eventually divorced after forty-nine years of marriage, and the dam of secrecy and denial slowly began to break.

Due to her upbringing and for other reasons, it was easy for Darci not to face the fact that something was terribly wrong in her life. She had learned the skill of avoiding her fears, faults, and heartbreak—and she was great at everything she set her heart on doing. She was so busy, made such good money, and had such a great social life, of course she was fine! She had no idea that denial and distraction were behaviors she was going to carry into every relationship—even her relationship with God.

While she pursued this path of willful self-destruction, Darci also saw a family who loved and cared for her, who refused to give up on her even when she was making them nuts by quitting school, living for the moment, being promiscuous, and constantly drinking. Her mother had been a strong Christian from the moment she had given her life to the Lord as a young girl at a Billy Graham crusade. Although Beverly didn't attend church for a while, she had a fervent prayer life and a close relationship with God. Her mother's faith was always in the back of Darci's mind, no matter where she was or what she was doing.

At times, Darci would come home drunk and cry to her mother that God was always speaking to her, even when she was doing stupid things. Beverly had reached a point where she was actually frightened that Darci's lifestyle would kill her, and she prayed even more fervently. In fact, it was the prayers of this tenacious mom that would prevail in the end.

One Sunday morning, Darci was lying in bed after a late night of bartending. Her mother came into her room and said she had a phone call. Darci pulled herself together to answer the call. It was her friend Kathy's mother, who had become an ordained minister. She said that God had awakened her in the night and told her to call Darci and ask her to read Jeremiah 29:11. Darci said, "Thanks.

I will." She hung up and rummaged around to find her Bible. She turned the pages that used to be so important to her and finally located the verse. She read, "For I know the thoughts that I think toward you, saith the LORD, thoughts of peace, and not of evil, to give you an expected end." She slammed the Bible shut in fear, believing that what she had just read meant she would die early. God was far, far away from her! There was nothing to do about it. Her bad decisions had brought her here and now she had to live with them.

If you had asked Darci what she wanted her life to look like, she would have said, "I want ten kids and to sing." She believed that was all she needed to be happy and successful in life. Kids and music. Although she was singing, she couldn't stay in a relationship with a man. At least one of her two desires had been realized, but she still needed to find a husband to have those kids.

Darci was an empty soul who believed her soul mate would complete her. He would give her the picture-perfect life she imagined, the picture-perfect life she thought she had had growing up and had lost. She had no idea she was simply a free spirit who had put herself in the chains of darkness and self-deception.

The Collision

When soul mates meet, there is often an incredible explosion in the hearts and minds of each. "This is it! I have found my partner for life! I love! I love! I love!" This happened to Darci and Danny for the first few months they knew each other. Then suddenly the wonderful explosion turned into a disastrous collision of two very needy, mixed-up people.

They had certain expectations of each other, and none of those expectations were being met. Still, something deep inside each of them knew they had found their soul mate. The problem was, their souls were sick. So they pressed on, determined to make each other well.

No matter what they tried, however, they made each other worse.

Love at First Sight

In June of 1992, when Darci was twenty-one and living in the fast lane, her dance team director was given the responsibility of putting together an all-city talent show for the Oklahoma City Fourth of July Celebration. Her director wanted Darci to sing and perform two numbers. Darci was in her element — and she was about to meet the love of her life.

Danny's father had convinced him to try out for the same show. Charlie was going to read some of his poetry, and he thought this would be a good opportunity to get Danny playing his music again — and get him out of his room! So they arrived outside the dance studio, where the auditions were being held, and Danny sat down with his guitar to practice. That's when Darci, hung over from the night before, arrived with her friend Hui Cha. They saw this "gorgeous, dark-haired, muscle-bound, sexy, guitar-playing stud" — and immediately began competing for his attention. Darci remembers trying to play it cool. She let her friend take the lead and start talking to Danny, but it wasn't long before she was drawn into the conversation.

Both of the women who approached Danny were pretty, but after he heard her sing at the first rehearsal, there was only Darci. She was a knockout! And she was so full of life. He didn't think he had a chance with her, though. He thought, *She's amazing! Even if I could get her to go out with me, I'd surely screw it up before long.*

Both Danny and his dad were accepted into the show. During the course of the rehearsals the following week, the sparks flew between Danny and Darci. At the time, Darci was incredibly busy. She had never quit working at the sports grill and was now a bartender there, along with dancing for the pro basketball team and working as the lead singer of karaoke at Oklahoma City's premier piano bar.

Danny was also busy. After PC Quest deserted him, he began working with his father in his land surveying business again, and he went back to school to get his degree in music education. Where they differed at that time was in their social lives. Darci had an active social life, while Danny generally spent his free time holed up in his bedroom, not wanting to even think about the music business. Meeting Darci and doing the show with her was just what he needed to get him out in the world again.

They would sit together in the bleachers and flirt when they weren't rehearsing. Occasionally she would irritate him, like asking for a drink of his water, then mischievously drinking the rest. At one point he thought, *If this girl doesn't stop, I'm gonna stick this water bottle in her ear!* But the irritation didn't last long. When Darci was rehearsing, Danny was in awe. There was no one else on the stage. And there was something dangerously and irresistibly exciting about her. Even when she made him angry, he was strangely drawn to her.

Darci asked Danny to come to the karaoke bar, and he and his father came. Danny wanted to show her that he was interested, but he was still unsure whether she liked him as much as he liked her. Everyone had a great time, and Danny and his dad were so impressed with Darci's charismatic way with the audience. She lit up the place.

As the Fourth of July show came to an end, Danny and Darci stood backstage talking, both feeling this incredible pull towards the other. Darci just knew Danny was going to ask her out, but he didn't. He only said that he would come to visit her at the karaoke bar again. Disappointed and confused, she began to walk away. Then something inside her said, "Go back. Give him one more chance." So she turned around, walked back, and pretended to look for a lost earring.

At that point, Danny knew it was now or never. He took a deep breath and asked, "Would you like to go out for dinner sometime?"

Darci looked up and said, "Sure, that would be great." With a mischievous smile, she took his hand and wrote her number on it. Then she turned and walked away on clouds. She thought about how handsome he was, and how easy it was to talk to him. She had no problem attracting men because of being a dancer and having a good figure, but that was the problem. In the end, they all seemed interested only in her body. Danny seemed different. He was confident, but he was also timid towards her. Maybe he liked her for more than her body. Maybe he even thought she was pretty.

Of course, Danny thought Darci was the most beautiful girl he had ever seen, and he couldn't believe she might be interested in him. He was amazed that when he got up the courage to ask her out, she had said yes! He immediately began to plan the best date he could think of, and from that first date, they were inseparable.

Not Exactly What They Expected

Their first date was July 13, 1992, which was Darci's parents' anniversary. She believes Danny was thirty minutes early, and that is why she wasn't ready, but he will argue he was right on time! They went to dinner and talked and talked. He had packed an ice chest with champagne and strawberries, so afterward they went to Lake Thunderbird. They drank and talked some more. At two in the morning, when he started to take her home, they got into another riveting conversation and ended up sitting in the park in Darci's neighborhood (she was staying at her mother's house).

She saw that he was intelligent, creative, and funny. He saw that she was a good listener, knew just what to say to make him feel good about himself, and was obviously very smart and talented. They both loved people. They both loved to drink and party. And most of all, they both loved music and performing.

Today, Darci isn't sure whether she decided this somewhat shy man needed a push or that she just couldn't help herself, but she leaned over and kissed him. Danny was blown away and easily kissed her back. After that, he took her home. That first, passionate kiss was the perfect ending to a perfect first date.

Darci came through the front door a little before five in the morning, just when her mother was getting up for work. She felt like she was floating. She walked to the bathroom, where she could hear water running, and leaned in the doorway to tell her mother, "Well, I met the guy I'm going to marry." Her mother was astonished because Darci had never talked about a man she dated that way, much less after the first date. She poured out everything she knew about him. They were definitely attracted to one another, but they also had a genuine friend connection. And he was so real and passionate about things! They both had close families, and she loved the fact that he helped his parents, worked with his dad, and always had something going on in his life.

Danny returned home just to count the hours before he thought he could call Darci, and he didn't wait long! They went out for seventeen days in a row, and after Danny brought her home, he would call her and they would talk until they fell asleep with their phones at their ears. Their first kiss had sealed their fate, and both families seemed to know it. Danny's father asked Danny and Darci to perform together at festivals and other gatherings where he read his poetry. They would go fishing at Uncle Kenneth's pond all night. In August, Danny's family threw a birthday party for him, and Darci's gift to him was a ticket to Las Vegas for her cousin's wedding. They stayed at the Excalibur with her parents, and everyone had a fantastic time.

The dancing coach put Darci on suspension for gaining weight, so she decided she had had enough and quit dancing for the basketball team. She thought she would have more time to spend with Danny, but he had joined a band called Unleash the Dog. They played gigs every weekend, and Darci could see how much Danny loved writing and performing music. She came to see him when she could and was proud of what he was doing, but she didn't like the way it was affecting their social life. Off and on she tried going back to school, but she could never stick with it. She often felt lonely, even with such a great boyfriend.

Danny plunged into his music again, as Unleash the Dog recorded their first CD, and his perfect new love with Darci began to unravel. In the beginning they had fun drinking and talking about music, about their friends and family, and about what they wanted in the future. More and more, however, they would get drunk and fight. She would bring up getting married, and he would say, "I'm not getting married until I'm thirty. I have to get the band established first." This was a maxim he had adopted from a high school teacher he respected, who had told him, "Danny, you don't really know who you are until you are thirty years old. Don't marry someone too soon. You might wake up and have changed and not be happy."

As 1993 dawned, Danny also had become really worried about Darci's drinking. He prided himself on being able to hold his liquor and stay in control, but to him, Darci was off the charts. When they would drink, she became uncontrollable, and he liked his life to be under his control. In one sense, her wild behavior excited him, but at the same time it terrified him. He never knew what she would say or do while she was drinking. Then he witnessed something that frightened him to death. One night they were drinking and Darci blacked out.

Instead of telling her how much she had scared him, that he was afraid she might die, and confronting her with how her personality changed when she drank, Danny was more afraid Darci would break up with him. So he began to manipulate her to try to get her to drink less or to keep her from drinking. It seemed hypocritical for him to continue drinking and tell her to stop, so he stopped taking her to places or to parties where there was the possibility they would drink. He buried himself even more in his music and the band, and when they were together he wanted to stay home. In this lifestyle, he began to gain weight again.

To Darci, Danny seemed to turn into an old man overnight. He didn't want to go to parties or to hang out with her friends in the bar where she worked. In fact, he seemed jealous of her friends and got angry when she wanted to party with them. He didn't want to go anywhere with her, and the old feelings of being different and not feeling beautiful haunted her again. More and more, all they would do is hang out in his room or her room and watch television or movies and eat. She was totally confused about what was going on. Where was the romantic and fun man she had fallen in love with? Obviously, he wasn't who she thought he was; or worse, he didn't care about her the way she thought he did.

Instead of manipulating her into drinking less, Danny's behavior drove Darci to spend even more time with her friends partying at the bar. When he would give in so he could remain a part of her life, they would get drunk together and usually fight about stupid things.

Both of their families were upset with them. Darci's parents liked Danny as a person, but they did not approve of their dating lifestyle. Although Darci wasn't doing anything different with Danny than she had done before she had met him, they had hoped he would help her to settle down. Instead, she seemed to be getting worse. One weekend, Danny took her to Dallas, and that was the last straw for Quint McBride. When they returned home, Quint was still in his underwear in the living room. He jumped up as they came through the front door and yelled, "How dare you take my daughter out of town and spend the night with her in a hotel!"

Danny thought Quint was crazy. At that time in their life, they both had bought into the world's belief that men and women could have sex whenever they felt it was right, and Danny saw nothing wrong with them spending the night together, in town or out of town, especially since he and Darci loved each other so much. He looked at Quint with disbelief and could only answer, "What do you mean?"

The two men raised their voices until they ended up nose to nose, Darci's father in his underwear, both ready to come to blows. Darci and her mother were upset and feeling helpless. Finally, Danny said, "I don't have to listen to this *%#!" and left. It caused a huge rift between Danny and Quint for some time. That night Danny wondered if he wanted to continue dating Darci, if it meant he had to deal with her father.

Darci's relationship with Danny's family was no better. Except for Danny's father, the family did not want to accept her. Danny believed they were threatened by her. After all, she had stolen his heart. When he was obsessed with computer games, fishing, music, sports, and eating, he was still theirs. But now he was obsessed with Darci! He didn't belong to them anymore. He rarely spent time with them, and if he did, she was usually there too. They were glad he was pursuing his music again, but that had nothing to do with her as far as they were concerned.

Things were about to get worse, although no one would know it.

Another Obsession Takes Root

When the Remington Park racetrack celebrated its five-year anniversary, Darci's family went to the track and invited Danny to go with them. They encouraged Danny to make a bet or two for fun. He lost about thirty dollars, which irritated him, but the whole process of gambling intrigued him. His only experience with it had been the occasional bet over a football game or playing poker with his friends, but the atmosphere at the racetrack was exciting.

No one saw this new addiction coming, particularly Danny. A few weeks later, as he was driving home from school, he decided to go to Remington Park simply on a whim. He bought a tip sheet and made a $10 trifecta bet, for which you have to correctly predict the first-, second-, and third-place winners in order. He won $750! That night he took Darci out and they partied. He paid off the $500 balance on his credit card, which was like a million dollars to him at the time. He liked this gambling thing and, like everything else he did, he was positive he could become good at it.

They had such a good time that night, Darci thought Danny was back to his old self. In the days that followed, however, she saw less and less of him. She didn't know he was spending more and more time at the racetrack. He got to know the local racing junkies and learned from the best of them how to pick winners. He began to improve and make a little money. He thought, *Maybe I could be a professional gambler.*

Danny was making so many trips to the track, he got tired of parking way out in the back lot. There was an area called "Preferred

Parking" for the VIPs, and he noticed their cars had tickets with colored numbers on them in the windows. He studied the pattern they used for the colors and numbers, then went to a copy shop and made his own tickets on the computer. He successfully forged Preferred Parking passes! Danny's gambling had escalated to recklessly breaking rules.

Now, when he was around his family, Danny felt like he was accomplishing something they couldn't. He would smile inside at his secret triumph. He was getting better and better at picking winners and believed he was in complete control, even when he lost money. He could not see the truth: His compulsive betting always left him in the negative numbers because he would not stop after he won.

The only part of his life that seemed to resist his control was Darci. Despite his efforts, she would drink and usually get drunk. He repeatedly warned her not to drink and drive, but she paid no attention. One night they met at a party in a small town. Darci got drunk as usual, and Danny told her not to drive. He told her that the police in that town looked for people who were speeding or driving recklessly, so he would drive her home. She left without telling him, and the next thing he knew, he was bailing her out of jail. She had been arrested for driving under the influence, commonly referred to as a DUI. For the next six months, he took her to work because her license was suspended and she didn't want her parents to know.

He would get so angry at her. Why did she keep doing this? Maybe the DUI and the daily reminder of it while he drove her to work would wake her up to her self-destructive behavior. What

Danny didn't see was that he was a making the problem worse, and what Darci did not understand was that she was resisting Danny's control just as she had her father's. For the most part, she used alcohol to kill the pain of feeling unloved, unwanted, and used. She had never recovered from the trauma of losing her virginity and being promiscuous. She was repressing all the little indications that her family was not the perfect family she wished it to be. And her Christian upbringing haunted her. She felt like the way she was living was an embarrassment to herself, to her parents, and to God. Whenever these thoughts surfaced, the shame and guilt were too much, so she just drank more.

Danny thought he was helping by trying to keep Darci away from situations where she could get into trouble, trying to get her to stay home as much as possible. When this was unsuccessful, he would throw her disapproving looks and sulk when she drank. All his attempts to control her simply gave her more excuses to drink. They were doing a dance of self-destruction.

Engagement Saves the Day?

Both families watched as the relationship became more and more stormy. When her boss at the karaoke bar made a pass at her, Darci told Danny. He went to the bar and threatened to "whoop his butt," challenging him to come out in front of his customers. Darci's boss refused, Danny called him a very bad name, and Darci quit. Now her only job was working as a bartender at the sports grill. Meanwhile, Danny was consumed with the band and spending all his free time at the track. He was cutting more and more of his classes. Their "dates" consisted of staying home. In his mind, he was keeping Darci safe. She was hurt, frustrated, and confused. What had happened to the guy from that first date?

Things came to a head in 1994, after Darci took a trip to San Francisco to visit her cousin for two weeks. Darci was very unhappy, had no passion for anything, and had no idea what to do with her life. In California, she had an amazing time and loved the area. When she returned, she had a new lease on life.

After Danny asked Darci to marry him, "the lie" began to take hold of him, the lie that said he couldn't support a wife and family doing what he loved to do. Being a music teacher didn't pay very much, so one semester shy of getting his degree in music education (all he had to do was student teach), he quit. The ulterior motive, of course, was that school was keeping him from going to the racetrack. His family was not pleased, but Danny had convinced himself and sought to convince them that he was doing the responsible "man thing." He could make a lot more money working with his father in the land surveying business. And besides, he was still playing with Unleash the Dog. It wasn't like he had given up music altogether.

One morning after Danny had spent the night with Darci, they were awakened by a phone call from his dad. He asked Danny to go by the Federal Building and pick up some FEMA flood maps. In a foul mood, Danny told him he would pick him up and they would go together. His father got angry and said, "I'll just go get them myself!"

Not long after that, Danny and Darci heard and felt a terrific explosion. Danny cried to Darci, "Hit the dirt!" and they both dropped to the floor in her living room. They thought the gas station nearby had blown up, but they soon learned it had not. Later, driving back to his parents' house to shower and change, Danny saw smoke rising from the downtown area. When he arrived home, he turned on the television and learned that the Federal Building had been bombed. It was April 19, 1995, the day Timothy McVeigh bombed the Murrah Building in Oklahoma City. Danny's heart cried, "My dad is there!" He thought that because of his selfishness, he had gotten his father killed.

Just then he heard a truck drive up. He ran outside to see his father in the driver's seat, grimly chewing tobacco. He had gone to the store to get some tobacco and decided to wait on Danny instead of going by himself. Danny thought, *This is the only time I've been thankful Dad chews tobacco!*

The summer wore on and the wedding was coming upon them in September. Danny grew more and more agitated about being responsible like his father had always been, so in August he did something that infuriated Darci and further confused his family. He quit the band. He told them he was sick of trying to make it in the music business and needed to focus on Darci and having a family.

Darci was completely baffled. Why would he quit something he loved doing and was really good at? Yet he insisted this was the right thing for both of them. August 13th was his last gig with Unleash the Dog, and it was his 26th birthday. Darci was sure Danny's heart must be aching, and it was. He couldn't believe he was breaking up the band, but he had to do the responsible thing like his father had. He would let go of his dream in exchange for a new life with Darci, who watched in silent anger and confusion.

Darci resigned herself to Danny's strange decisions, but she was clueless about his involvement with gambling. She did like it when he won money from "betting every now and then." A couple of months after they were engaged, Danny had won a small fortune with which to begin their new life. He had put down a $4 bet and won $148,263.80. It made the local newspaper, the *Sunday Sun*, on November 13, 1994:

> The garage sale at the Cahill house wasn't quite as important Friday as it seemed it would be when dad Charlie and son Danny took a day off from the family surveying business to set things up.
>
> Late Thursday afternoon, the sixth horse on one of the nine $4 Pick Six tickets the two had purchased early on Thursday won in the eighth race at Remington Park and the Cahills, along with five other winners, were $148,263 richer.
>
> "We were keeping up with the results as the day went along and every time we won a race, it became a little less important to price the stuff for the garage sale," Charlie Cahill said with a snicker. "We didn't find out we had won for sure until we saw all the numbers on the news."
>
> In fact, Charlie Cahill, a Cowboy poet who often provides his verse for the *Sun's* "Poetry Corner," said Friday morning he still didn't really believe it.

"I'm sitting here holding this ticket and looking at the numbers, but I won't believe we won until I've got something else in my hands," he said.

The elder Cahill credited his son's know-how and past experience in handicapping horses at Remington Park over the last three years and some good fortune for making their Pick Six dream come true.

"It was his skill and my luck," Charlie said with another snicker.

Charlie was proud of Danny's "skill" and had no idea what an addiction gambling had become in his son's life. He did not have a problem with it, so he didn't see it in anyone else. He also loved Darci, and was pleased that they had this money to begin their new life. When several other family members and friends said they thought Darci was marrying him for his money, Danny pointed out the obvious: She had said yes before he won at the track!

Although Darci was oblivious to Danny's newfound love for gambling, there was one time she wondered about it. When he was still in school and supposed to be in class, she had gone to the track to place some bets for her boss and saw him there. He had a perfectly logical explanation, however. No one knew how addicted he was. Not only was it one of the reasons he quit school, but he also skipped Grandpa Charlie's funeral for a trip to Las Vegas he had already paid for!

As the wedding drew closer, Danny continued to gain weight. By the day of the wedding, he weighed 275 pounds. His best friend and best man David said, "What the heck! You were supposed to lose weight for the wedding not gain weight!" Nevertheless, after an eventful engagement, on September 23, 1995, Danny and Darci were married.

The wedding was filled with disappointments for both of them. Little girls grow up with images of themselves walking down the aisle to meet their Prince Charming, and Darci was meeting a severely overweight man who didn't seem to love her for herself. At this point she was so broken inside, she really didn't know what to think. The only thing she knew for sure was that she still believed in the man she had met that summer in 1992, sitting outside the dance studio, playing his guitar, with such great passion and dreams. He was still in there somewhere!

Meanwhile, Danny was upset about a lot of details that all seemed to point to disaster for their marriage. They had wanted to be married in his family's Episcopal church, the beautiful and majestic St. Paul's Cathedral downtown, but the bombing of the Murrah Building had also blown the roof off of it. As a result, they had to be married in another Episcopal church in Oklahoma City, one that was not nearly as beautiful.

Darci, always consumed with her friends and having many of them, had seven bridesmaids. Seven! Danny scrambled to find enough men friends to match them, which he did. But the worst happened when the priest Danny had been raised under, who was presiding at the wedding, called Darci "Keri" and messed up parts of the wedding ceremony. Danny knew his priest was older and had just buried his sister, but it was a bitter pill to swallow nonetheless.

Then came the reception. Danny and Darci were so busy that they never had anything to eat. After all that planning and looking forward to the food (especially Danny), they were to receive "to-go" boxes, which they never received because someone stole them. As they went up to their room at the hotel, hungry and tired, Danny consoled himself that at least it was their wedding night, and he expected great things to happen. Unfortunately, Darci was in a state of emotional turmoil, and the last thing she wanted to do was make love. When Danny made his move, she moved away and said, "I just can't do this right now."

This was the last straw for Danny, who was screaming inside, *What is going on here?!!! I marry the girl and she doesn't want to sleep with me on our wedding night!* Again, he wondered if he had done the right thing. The whole wedding seemed to point to a big mistake.

Something changed after they got to Florida for their honeymoon. They flew into Orlando and rented a car, which they drove to a condo in New Smyrna Beach. Darci's aunt owned it and gave it to them for two weeks. It was in a great location, near the beach. They visited the pier to eat fresh shrimp, cooked just the way they liked it, and drank pitchers of beer. They spent two days at Disney World, where Darci had Danny take a picture of her with Tigger, her favorite Winnie the Pooh character. At Epcot they ate foods from almost every country, and by the end of the day they were miserably full. Danny looked at Darci and said, "We could be an anti-acid commercial right now!"

They rode bikes to the beach, and they ate at all the places Darci's aunt had suggested, which were fabulous. They drove along the coast of Florida, seeing all the sights and having a wonderful time talking and laughing. At one point they saw a billboard a long way down the road that said GAMBLING in huge letters. Danny was excited as they approached the sign, and then they read the small print underneath: "Have a problem? Call 1-800-GAMBLER for help." Suddenly Danny was quiet. Darci was still clueless.

Because there wasn't a lot of drinking, Danny was more at ease. He mistakenly reasoned that Darci's drinking problems were caused by how she was being treated or whether or not she was happy. He believed if she was happy with him and with her circumstances, she wouldn't want to drink. That's why marrying her was the key. That would make her happy, and she would stop drinking. This was a lie, of course, and it set both of them up for failure in the days to come.

There were a couple of times they both drank too much together and everything was great, but this was soon forgotten. The challenge was to keep Darci happy and limit what she drank. Danny reasoned that the alcohol itself was doing something to her physically. She was like the Kim Basinger character in the movie Blind Date, who would be just fine until she had a certain amount of alcohol, at which point she would become an out-of-control drunk. So not only did he try to keep her happy, but also he continued to try to limit how much they drank.

One night at the pier, Danny asked the band to play a song, but they refused. Undaunted, he put a twenty-dollar bill on the music stand and said, "Let me play and let Darci sing. You won't be disappointed." The bandleader allowed them to perform, and the crowd went wild. The band asked them to sing again later in the evening, which they did. However, they had had too much to drink and their performance wasn't quite as sharp. Still, the band wanted them to come back and perform that Friday night. They didn't, but it was an awesome experience to perform together again.

There were moments when they laughed at being "Okies," who were showing their lack of class. At an upscale restaurant one evening, Danny noticed escargot on the menu. When the waiter came, he said, "Escargot, please."

The waiter looked at him quizzically and asked, "Just one?"

Since one order was fifteen dollars, Danny swallowed and stuck to his order. When the waiter had gone, he leaned toward Darci and said, "Is there just a single snail on a plate? Oh my gosh! What if he just brings us one snail? That would be so embarrassing!"

The waiter returned with a bowl of garlic butter on a plate surrounded by five snails. Danny and Darci burst out laughing, and the waiter walked away shaking his head.

An elderly couple at a table near theirs noticed them and struck up a conversation. They were celebrating their anniversary of many years. The lady talked about what a difference it made when God was the head of your marriage. This wasn't the only time the subject of God came up.

One day at the beach, the waves were huge because hurricane Opal was on its way. Still, they had a great time in the ocean. The next day at Sea World, Darci's leg began to burn badly. They told her she had been stung by a jellyfish. This was just before they left to return to Oklahoma, and their flight was the last to leave before hurricane Opal hit. It was one of the roughest flights they had ever taken—and their foul language didn't go unnoticed.

The people sitting in front of Danny and Darci turned around to see who was doing all the swearing. They had a look of surprise on their faces as they recognized Darci and she recognized them. She had grown up with their kids, and they were church people! Later they told Darci's mother that after they recognized Darci, they began to pray for God to intervene in her marriage and their lives. They had had some experience with the path Danny and Darci were travelling and knew God was the only one who could help them avoid catastrophe and heartache.

God was using different people to say to Danny and Darci, "Look, I'm here for you when you are ready."

A Marriage Only God Could Save

Back in Oklahoma City, they settled into married life. After several years of spending nights together and dating, living together turned out to be a completely different experience. Danny thought that marrying Darci would do the trick. That's what she wanted. That's what he had done. So now she should be happy and stop staying out late getting drunk with friends. Darci thought that marriage would change Danny. He would lose weight. He would spend more time with her and give her the attention she deserved. He would take her out and party with her again, and they would perform together, like they did on their honeymoon.

Both were sorely disappointed. Before they were married they had put up with each other's problems. Now that they were married, and after a few weeks proved the other person was not changing, they were afraid they had to live with all these problems for the rest of their lives. Each of them spiraled downward, turning to their addictions and bad habits for relief and comfort.

About a month after they were married, Danny was listening to Dr. Laura on the radio. A woman called in and said, "My husband stays out all night and drinks with his buddies on the weekends. He also stays late at the bar with them after work."

Dr. Laura replied, "Did he do this before you married him?"

"Yes," answered the lady.

"Then why did you marry him? People always marry those who do things they don't like, believing they will change when they are married. That never happens. You shouldn't have married him if you didn't like what he was doing when you were dating."

Danny was struck by this idea. Maybe it was true. Maybe Darci would never stop drinking. He said to himself, "This stinks and she's not changing." Their problems only encouraged him to eat and gamble more. Darci knew Danny was eating too much because she could see the weight gain, but she still had no idea he was gambling. He carefully controlled their finances and paid all the bills. All she knew was that they never seemed to have enough money.

The weight gain made it more difficult for Danny to go anywhere with Darci socially. It also strained their sexual relationship. She continued to work at the sports bar, usually still staying out late with her friends after hours. Since she was the bartender, she could have her own personal parties and forget her obese and emotionally absent husband was at home waiting for her.

Danny worked hard at his job, eating and gambling and worrying about Darci's drinking all the while. He began to wonder if she would ever stop. He considered quitting smoking because he didn't want to get sick, and Darci didn't let him smoke in their house anyway. However, in addition to being addicted to cigarettes, he had always heard that quitting them would make you gain weight, and that excuse was all he needed to continue his destructive behavior.

By February of 1996, Danny and Darci had been married almost six months and were nothing more than roommates. The only time they spent together was on Friday or Saturday night, when they went to a local pub. Danny would join the weekly poker tournament, and Darci would arrive later. After he finished playing poker, they would get together with their friends, usually ending up at a local "greasy spoon" to devour a big breakfast or burgers and fries in the middle of the night.

During the work-week they were rarely together. Although Darci came home drunk in the middle of the night many times, and sometimes had to be driven home by her friends, she was never unfaithful to Danny. He questioned it a few times, but his routine could have caused her to question him as well. After work he would come home to play video games, have a smoke, and eat. Then he would leave again. He was gambling, but Darci didn't know that. All she knew was that he avoided her, so she avoided the reality of their life together by staying away and being with her friends.

At this point, Danny and Darci had no real connection or intimacy. They were ships passing in the night—but the day was about to dawn.

The Music Hook

We know that a prayer of someone who loves you and believes God can do the impossible is the greatest power on earth. No doubt Darci and Danny's families and every Christian they knew were praying that the couple would exhaust their own abilities and efforts, come to the end of themselves, and realize they needed help from Someone a lot smarter than they were. There is no other explanation as to why they found themselves in church one day.

Darci and Danny quickly discovered that doing life with Jesus didn't mean it was easier, but He was there to help as He began to lead them out of their mess.

Darci Goes "Fanatic"

Change began when Darci attended a baby shower for her friend Kathy, who was pregnant with her second child and now living in Tulsa. Darci had fun seeing old friends, Kathy's family, and a few women from the church in Oklahoma City where Kathy's mother ministered. One particular lady named Carol discerned what a desperate, lost soul Darci was, and after the shower she asked

Kathy about her. Carol told Kathy that God had put something in her heart to speak to Darci.

The following week, Kathy called and asked Darci to visit her mother's church on Friday night, and for some reason Darci said yes. It might have been because she and Danny had grown apart in the first months of marriage. They were living separate lives.

From the moment Darci walked into the church, she was overwhelmed by the powerful presence of God, and His love began to melt her cold, hard heart. The praise and worship music soothed her tormented soul, and then Kathy's friend Carol walked over to her. Carol leaned in and whispered things only God could have known about Darci's life; dreams she had in her heart that she hadn't shared with others; things that had made her feel guilty and ashamed. She told Darci how much God loved her and how He had forgiven her. Then she told Darci that God only wanted her to surrender to Jesus and make Him Lord over her life. She could be forgiven and cleansed of all the guilt and shame of her past and be free to live the life He had for her.

Although Carol was doing the talking, Darci didn't hear her voice. God was whispering in her ear. It was as if they were the only ones in the room, and each word He said made her more and more alive. With tears streaming down her face, she gave her heart to Jesus and felt the weight of the world roll off her shoulders. All her fears of dying young and childless disappeared as He told her she would have children and fulfill her purpose. Inside she felt whole and clean and thoroughly and completely loved—really loved. She realized she had spent her life believing so many lies, and the main one was that anyone or anything other than Jesus could truly satisfy her need to be loved. Now she knew only He could fill her soul with peace and joy.

It was June 1996 when Darci walked into her home and stood before Danny radically changed. He had no idea what to think when he looked up and heard what she had to say. She said, "Well, I gave my life to Jesus tonight and everything's going to be different! I feel so free! I know He loves me, and I know what I'm supposed to do. I'm going to be a music minister and sing for God!"

Danny's entire being recoiled in horror. Panic mode set in. "No way am I going to live with a preacher! Are you insane? You're talking like one of those crazy fanatics!"

Darci realized how strange she must have appeared to Danny, but she was undeterred. "I don't care what you think or what you say. I know this is real. I know God is going to show me a whole new way to live."

"Yeah, whatever!" And for several weeks, Danny observed the "new" woman he was living with. Yes, she seemed happier, and there was this indescribable peace about her, but would it last?

When people first give their lives to Jesus, some may have a miraculous experience and lose all desire for a certain self-destructive behavior. However, they will find that it isn't always that easy to get rid of a problem in their lives. Eventually they will have to do what all believers do: put their hand in Jesus' hand and follow Him, and He will help them become more and more free from sin along the way.

"Sin" is actually a great word because it simply means that we miss the mark; we veer off the right path into the wrong path. When we do, we hurt ourselves, and sometimes the people around us. Sometimes we grieve the heart of God as well. And truly, all sin is selfish and self-centered.

When we realize we have sinned, we repent, which is another great word. It simply means to change your mind and change direction. When you sin, you get off the right path; when you repent, you get back on the right path. Of course, when a person comes to Jesus, there is this "knowing" that they are unable to overcome their sin alone and need help. Then Jesus comes into their heart, and they have no desire to go in the wrong direction. They repent and turn their lives onto the right path—with Him.

What they discover later is that this isn't a one-time deal!

Inside, Darci was radically changed in her spirit, and deep inside she felt right with God; but her soul—her mind, emotions, and will—still had a lot of learning to do. She had spent years drinking to release all her pent-up emotions. Now she needed to find out who she was in Christ and allow Him to deal with her emotional problems. On some level of understanding, she knew she was abusing alcohol, but it would take some time for her to see that truth, accept it, and then receive the strength from God she needed to stop the abuse.

The real turning point came when Danny was awakened in the middle of the night by a loud knock on the door. He looked at the clock. It was 4 a.m. *Great, this is where the highway patrol tells me Darci has been killed.* He opened the door to find her being propped up by a strange woman. By the way she was dressed, it was obvious she was a prostitute. The woman was half out of her mind with rage and blurted out her story, half in English, half in Spanish, while Danny got Darci to the bedroom and into bed.

Darci had wrecked her car near a hotel in a bad part of town. Then she was robbed, and the prostitute came to her aid. If the prostitute had not rescued her, Darci probably would have been raped, killed, or both. Always good in a crisis, Danny took the woman back to her hotel, thanked her, and gave her some money for her trouble. Then he called a tow truck, and once the car was home, he crawled wearily back into bed as the sun came up. Darci woke up.

Danny had reached the end of his patience with her and said, "Something's got to change, or we need to get an attorney and file for divorce."

That's when Darci said what he didn't want to hear, "I want to go back to church." The last thing he thought he needed was church, but if it would keep her from drinking, he would do it. He would try anything! To maintain control over the situation, however, he insisted they go to his Episcopal church. Darci agreed, but it didn't last long. After one service she said, "I can't do this. I want us to try my church."

Culture Shock

Danny wanted nothing to do with Darci's church, so she began going by herself. "Her church" was only a couple of years old, located in downtown Oklahoma City. The pastor was none other than Darci's old pastor, who had fallen years ago; but his marriage and ministry had since been restored. The congregation was multicultural—white, black, brown, and everything in between—and the music was fantastic. They had a great band, choir, praise and worship leaders, and a lot of talented vocal and instrumental soloists. The combination of the music and the preaching and teaching from her pastor and other gifted ministers made Darci feel like she was experiencing heaven on earth.

One week, Darci came home and announced that she had prayed and was now speaking in tongues. Speaking in tongues! Danny felt like she had turned into an alien being. While Darci felt like she was in heaven, he felt like he had died and gone to hell. He did not recognize her anymore and couldn't relate to half the things she said.

Danny felt like an outsider to Darci's new life, and he had no desire to be a part of it either. He did not need God like that. He thought attending a normal church like his was just fine. She was deluding herself, or she needed something he didn't need. The only good part about it was that she wasn't staying out to drink like before—and, of course, she seemed happier. There were times when Danny was jealous of her faith.

Darci was ecstatic about her new relationship with God and her new church, but more than anything she wanted to share it all with Danny. No matter how much she asked, Danny would not go with her; so she asked God to show her how to pray for him. She longed for him to know Jesus personally and for them to follow him together.

She began laying her hands on Danny when he was asleep at night, praying that he would want to go to church with her. She just knew that once he got through the church doors, God would do the rest. Finally, after about six weeks of this, Danny got up with her one Sunday morning and said, "Okay, I'll go with you." He thought, *Church or Darci coming home drunk? I'll take church.*

At the beginning of the service, there was a special performance. Dancers with flags came bounding down the aisles to recorded music. They continued dancing at the front and around the church. Danny was in complete culture shock. Dancing in church? What the heck is this?! This was not like the church he grew up in at all. He began to count the minutes until it would be over and they could get out of there. He was never coming back to this crazy place again!

Darci knew Danny was probably freaking out, and she wasn't wrong. Just then the dancing ended and the band walked through a door and took the stage. Danny elbowed Darci, and she was afraid he was going to tell her he wanted to leave. Instead, he pointed to the bass player. It was his friend, Will, a well-known and respected musician in the clubs around town. Darci remembered meeting him a couple of years ago, except then he was in bright purple, spandex biker shorts! She knew Danny had played in clubs with him many times. When Danny saw Will, he thought, *What is he doing here?*

As the singing commenced, people stood and raised their hands, some of them doing this waving motion. They were singing songs with a rock beat, and they often clapped their hands and shouted. Then a beautiful blonde woman got up and belted out a hymn to

God. She obviously knew what she was doing and had a great voice. Darci knew she was part of a family of musicians and singers who had sung Gospel for many years, and she thanked God. Danny would need to hear some professional musicians for this church to be appealing.

After the service Will came down to greet them, giving Danny a warm hug. Then he said, "Danny, I don't get done playing the bar until 3 or 4 AM, so can you take over for me here at the church? They begin rehearsal at 8am and I get no sleep. Can you do that for me? I've been trying to find someone good enough to do it, and here you are!"

Although he had not touched his bass in over a year, Danny couldn't resist the offer to play music again—even if it was at this weird church. With some reservation, he went to rehearsal the next week and was surprised at how much he enjoyed it. He liked the people in the band, and the music minister obviously knew what she was doing. Several months later, Darci joined the praise and worship team. She was happy that she and Danny were not only performing together but also in church together every week. She knew Danny wasn't thrilled, but God had answered her prayer!

Danny began going to church to keep Darci from drinking, which seemed to be working—well, most of the time. At Danny's high school reunion that summer, they went out with everyone to a bar. Darci drank too much and began sharing Jesus with the others! Danny was a little freaked out to see her tell his high school friends about Jesus in that condition, and seeing her drunk again was unnerving; but in the months to come it was clear that she was leaving alcohol behind.

More and more, Danny stayed at the church for other reasons. Now he was there primarily because of the music. The musicians were first-rate, and the music really began to touch his heart. After all, it wasn't like he didn't believe in God!

Meanwhile, he was continuing to work with his father, gamble, eat too much, and was continually amazed at some of the things that were taught at the church. At least he and Darci could talk about some of it now. More than anything, they had hope for their marriage. The pastor and his wife were very open about how they had completely destroyed their life together by their own faults and failings, but God had restored them. Maybe God was the one who could put Humpty Dumpty back together again!

Danny and Darci slipped into a new routine that centered mostly on church activities. More and more, Danny felt comfortable with the services and the people he was meeting, especially the musicians. He began to feel the presence of God as they played and sang. The music softened his heart and opened his mind to embrace the truth he was hearing, and he liked the fact that he was encouraged to read and study the Bible for himself. In every service, he felt God getting closer and closer to him.

Like every human being, Danny was not looking for a religious system to tell him what to do and when to do it; he was looking for something alive and real when it came to the issue of God. He wanted to know Him, and he remembered that when he was nine, nearly every week he called an outreach of a local church called "Tell a Story." He would hear a story that was like a parable of the Gospel, and then there would be an invitation to pray the prayer to receive Jesus into your heart.

One week he called and heard a story about a mother, who was playing with a puppy and her toddler on the porch of their house. The phone rang and she stepped inside to take the call. While she was gone, a poisonous snake slithered onto the porch. It coiled to attack the child, but the puppy attacked the snake before it could strike, so the snake bit the puppy again and again. Then the snake bit the baby on the leg and glided off the porch.

The puppy died, but the baby lived because the snake had put all its venom into the puppy. By the time it bit the child, there was no venom left. The person on the phone explained that what the puppy did for that child is like what Jesus did for each of us on the cross. Danny realized the truth of the Gospel, the Good News that Jesus paid the price for his sins, and he prayed the prayer to receive Him as his Lord and Savior.

Although he had this initial salvation experience at nine years old, the church he was attending with his parents did not help him to grow in his relationship with the Lord. Danny was a very active and expressive kid, and the Episcopal Church traditions and liturgy were not something he could relate to, like his experience with Tell a Story. So by the age of thirteen, having forgotten his salvation experience, he told his parents he was not going to church with them anymore. They were upset with him, but shortly after this, the rector of their church was caught embezzling funds. This crushed his mother, both his parents became disenfranchised with the church, and the family stopped going to church altogether.

Danny's parents were believers, but they were quiet about their faith. His mother Sandy told him once that when she was fifteen and her father passed away, Jesus visited her in her backyard. His father considered faith a private matter, not to be yelled from the housetops. Charlie had turned to Jesus as a boy, when his home life was so distressing, and he would say that his faith had gotten him through that and all the other difficulties he had faced in life. He had read the Bible and talked with his children about different passages for years, but Danny was the youngest, and by the time he had his salvation experience, his dad had slowly stopped doing that.

From age thirteen, Danny had wondered if God was real. As an adult, he still had lots of questions. When he was picking his parents up from the airport after a trip to California, he sat in the car waiting, debating whether there even was a God. He thought, *What if it is all a big hoax?! What a waste!* But then, fear gripped him. He thought, *But what if He is real, and I'm sitting here denying Him?*

He turned the radio dial and heard, "What if you were floating in space and saw a wristwatch fly by? You saw the gears working and it kept perfect time. What are the odds of that just happening by chance?"

Danny thought, *There isn't a chance a watch could create itself. There has to be an inventor for those gears and everything.*

Then the man said, "The human eye is amazing. It makes a watch seem like a tinker-toy. Have you ever seen a cut heal? Have you ever seen the birth of a child? Why would anyone think a watch had to have a creator, but a human being just happened?"

Danny remembered seeing his newborn niece Danielle for the first time. He had looked at that miraculous new life, and his heart was sure God was real.

Now Danny was about to renew his relationship with the Lord—because he wanted to quit smoking. His father had smoked for years and was showing signs of breathing problems. Charlie had quit smoking and begun chewing tobacco, but the damage was already done. Danny was worried that he would gain more weight if he quit, but he was more afraid of dying from continuing to smoke.

During a revival at the church, he went up to the front for prayer, asking God to help him quit. It was March 1997, and Danny never smoked another cigarette again! Immediately he lost all desire to smoke, and he had no withdrawal symptoms. This miracle, that God loved him so much that He took all desire for smoking away and spared him the pains of withdrawal, was all Danny needed to surrender his life to Him. He made the kind of commitment that characterized all the turning points in his life.

Danny talked to the pastor. He told him about his history in the Episcopal Church, how he had prayed the prayer of salvation as a child and then slowly turned away from the faith. His pastor encouraged him to be baptized, which would signify his new relationship with the Lord.

In the Episcopal Church they baptize babies, so his mother believed he didn't need to be baptized again. Danny explained to her, "I didn't have a choice when I was a baby. Now I can choose, and it means something to me." Then she understood, and his parents attended his baptism the following Sunday.

They didn't care much for the pastor or the whole Charismatic experience, but they were glad Danny and Darci had found faith in Jesus. They were also encouraged by the positive changes that were already taking place in their lives. After the service, Danny's father told Danny that he was proud of him for being such a good man. Danny hadn't heard that from his father until that very moment.

Laying a New Foundation

So Danny and Darci embarked on a new adventure of faith. They began praying together at meals, and eventually they were more comfortable praying together about other issues in their lives or in the lives of other people. After awhile, they really enjoyed their times of prayer and were surprised at how intimate they became with one another through it. They started attending classes at the church on various subjects, and as members of the music team, they were at all the conferences and special meetings.

They talked about what they were learning about the Bible. They learned about giving to the church, not only with their time and talents but also with their money. They began to give whatever they could spare from their monthly income, and despite Danny's secret gambling, God blessed them in so many ways.

Without their realizing it, Darci's drinking ceased to be an issue that divided them. And something else of significance took place. They both realized that God had brought them together for a reason. He had a plan for their lives, things for them to accomplish for Him in the world together. They would need this understanding for what lay before them. Drinking and smoking were not the only things they had to lose!

Danny approached getting to know God the way he approached everything he was interested in: going two hundred miles an hour with everything in his being. He continued to eat too much and gain weight. He continued to gamble and work long hours in the land surveying business. But he was also active in the church, especially the music. As Danny praised and worshipped God through his gift of music, his heart opened up first to receive Jesus and thereafter to receive everything He had for him. Music made his soul come alive and kept it alive.

Danny and Darci were now united in their faith, and so changes began to happen rapidly. They began to think differently, and that changed the way they talked and how they behaved. Their hearts became tender and open to one another in a way they had never experienced before, even when they first met. They were applying everything they were learning about God's truth, and the most amazing things occurred when they prayed together. When they knew they were in agreement and that they were praying God's will, He moved miraculously on their behalf.

Compared to before they gave their lives to Jesus, the next couple of years were incredible. It was the difference between walking in darkness and walking in the light. The path seemed more and more clear. They began to really trust and confide in one another. If they questioned something, God saw to it that the next sermon addressed that issue. When they had an argument or conflict, instead of ignoring it or trying to manipulate one another, they generally dealt with it together in prayer.

Nevertheless, they were still "babies" in the faith, and life was not always a smooth ride. One morning they were asked to lead worship during the early service, just Danny on guitar and Darci singing. They got up late, rushed to get ready, and were almost out the door when Danny said, "Did you turn out the lights?"

Darci said, "I don't know, but we're late. Let's just go."

Danny flew into a rage, accusing her of not caring about anything he cared about. He was paying all the bills and she was just pouring his hard-earned money down a hole. He got so mad, he punched a hole in a wall, and Darci came back at him. They yelled, decided church was obviously a waste of time, and "went to their corners."

After awhile, they talked. They admitted that it was stupid to get that mad over who turned out the lights. They decided they should go to the second service. It would be embarrassing after missing the first, especially since they were supposed to lead worship, but they would go anyway.

What were the first words of the pastor's sermon? "Today we're going to talk about dealing with anger." That morning, they found God's grace in their weakness.

One day while praying, Darci believed God showed her that Danny had some pornography magazines and tapes from years before in his bottom drawer. She felt like God wanted her to get rid of them. She told Him, "I'll do this, but You're going to have to make it right with Danny. I'm afraid he's going to be mad, and these are his things and not mine to get rid of."

Sure enough, she found the pornography in the bottom drawer. She took it to a dumpster in another part of town left it there. The very next day, Danny came to Darci and said, "I need to talk to you about something." She had no idea what it was, and Danny told her that he felt God wanted him to get rid of the magazines and tapes in one of his drawers. Darci looked at him and smiled. They were excited that God was speaking directly to both of them as a married couple.

Darci told Danny that she really wanted to quit her job, and he was all for it. She was still bartending at the sports grill because God had told her to continue for a while longer. He said the people she knew there needed to see the difference He had made in her life—and they did! Her boss told her he had never seen anyone change so drastically. So they waited for the right time.

As she was being a witness at the bar, her desire to have children came to the forefront. Danny wasn't ready, of course. They were in debt because of his gambling losses, and although they were both working, he didn't make much and wasn't secure about adding the responsibility of a baby. He would just say, "I'm not ready. It's just not the right time."

He continued to believe he was in control of his gambling. He was hiding it from everyone, and he began to know for sure that it was wrong, but he still felt he could handle it by himself and keep it a secret from all the people he respected, particularly Darci and his family. They had no idea, and Darci kept praying God would bring in more money. Their bills were not so bad, and she often wondered where the money went.

Where was it going? Here is a typical example: One day, Danny went to the track with a friend and bet his entire paycheck. His friend freaked out when he realized what Danny had done. Lucky for Danny, he won enough to get back all but $3 of his pay. However, for the first time, his friend's reaction caused him to question whether or not he had a gambling problem. He shrugged it off and proceeded to place another bet! (It was a small one, however.)

Money often took Darci and Danny to the front of the church for prayer. On one particular Sunday, they said, "Please pray that Darci finds a different job." She wanted to quit bartending, and she knew it was time. She thought Danny would be upset because they needed the money, but he told her God was telling him the same thing. Again, they knew God was talking to them as one.

The pastor said, "Why don't we pray your job will go to the next level so that Darci can stay home with your children?"

Danny thought, *Wait, that's not what I asked for!* But at the same time, the light bulb went on in both their heads, that they could actually have that kind of life. They agreed in prayer with the pastor, and within a couple of weeks, Danny and his father were given a tremendous offer from Charlie's old boss. Together they went to work for him, which gave each of them more money than they had ever earned.

In fact, Charlie really didn't want to go to work for anyone else, but he knew he would be retiring in a few years and Danny needed to learn things about surveying that he just couldn't learn without working downtown. It was a wonderful and wise thing for Charlie to do, and ultimately this move would allow Darci to stay home and raise his grandchildren.

Danny had been helping his father in the land surveying business since he was nine, and he had continued working with his father off and on his entire life. Now he and his father agreed it was time he went to the next level. Although Danny's salary was much better in his new position, he made a deal with his new boss that he would receive a raise of $5,000 a year when he got his surveyor's license. The boss agreed, and Danny made good on his part of the deal. Because he grew up in the profession, he didn't have to go to school for a degree. He took the exam and passed both parts the first time, which was rare. At twenty-eight years old Danny became a licensed land surveyor, which was very young for someone without a degree in the field.

Even with all this success, planted in Danny's heart was a bitterness that would not come to the surface until years later. He was now doing a job he really did not want to do. He was playing music at church, but he wasn't writing songs. He felt angry that his fellow musicians had found some success while he had laid down his passion. He took some satisfaction that he was following in his hero's footsteps by working with his father, but he unknowingly resented it at the same time. This would be a source of anger for many years. "The lie" had taken full hold of his life, and to compensate, he ate whatever he wanted and gambled in secret. He gained more weight and was 330 pounds by the end of 1997.

Trusting God

After quitting her job at the sports grill, Darci prayed for some kind of work she could do that she would enjoy until she and Danny agreed it was time to have children. A friend from church, who had started a business cleaning and organizing houses, asked her to go to work for her. Never being the office type, Darci found she really enjoyed being physically active in her new line of work.

She cleaned for one family four days a week and grew to love them. The wife was diagnosed with breast cancer soon after she began working there, but Darci learned that it wasn't her first bout with the illness. That explained why the house was in chaos when Darci arrived the first day. It was a beautiful, historic home with three stories and a huge basement. The top floor had two large bedrooms and a full bath, yet it was crammed wall to wall with clothes, furniture, and other goods. The basement contained stacks and stacks of clothes. Darci felt that God literally anointed her to conquer this mountain of clutter. It took several months, but she washed all of the clothes, which she either donated to charity or put away. She organized all the closets and set the house in order as she cleaned. She would pray and sing songs to the Lord while she worked, and peace began to reign in the household.

She felt that God was teaching her how to pray for people. Since the family she worked for was consumed with caring for their sick wife and mother, she prayed for them often. She also tried to help with the things that were being neglected because of the lady's illness. One example stands out above the rest. Their son was doing a science project, in which he used little white mice. They were housed in a cage, but around the holidays she noticed the cage was gone.

A few months later, Darci was instructed to clean the pool house. The cage of mice was there. She was horrified to see that, with no food or water, the live mice were eating the dead ones! She told the father, and he said he would take care of it. The next week she found the mice starving again, so she bought food and set out water. A month later, when it was time to clean the pool house again, there were only two surviving mice laying flat on the bottom of the cage. She could see that they were barely breathing.

Growing up in the country, loving animals of all kinds for so many years, Darci was devastated. She sobbed and prayed, "Lord, I know I shouldn't care this much because they aren't humans, but I know You have a heart for Your creatures." Inside she heard the words, He cares for the birds of the air and beasts of the fields. Just then her faith seemed so big and she said, "Lord, You said if we lay hands on the sick they will recover. So I put my hand on this cage and believe that You will bring these mice back to life." At that moment, the mice began to move around! Darci was struck by the idea that there was nothing too small for God. He loved her, and He cared about what she cared about.

It wasn't long after she started cleaning and organizing houses that Darci felt it was time to bring up the baby issue again. This time Danny was okay with it, so they began to pray that she would become pregnant. Three months later, one early morning Darci decided to take a pregnancy test. She looked at the result and ran out of the bathroom to wake up Danny, "We're going to have a baby!" They were both elated, even with all the financial distress they were in, and began to plan for their baby's arrival. They didn't talk about the future; they just lived through each moment, savoring this special time. When they found out the baby was a boy, they were even more excited.

Darci continued to clean through her pregnancy, and God used her in her job. When she entered her fifth month, she began to tire, and it was harder and harder for her to climb stairs. Now she was really ready to stop working and stay home so that she could prepare for their baby and be a mom like she had always dreamed of being. This overwhelmed Danny. He wanted her to stay home, but their finances were still in disarray.

Danny's weight was also taking its toll physically. One day at work, he was about to pass out and called for help. Susan, a co-worker, came in and he told her he felt dizzy. She took his blood pressure and it was dangerously high, so she rushed him to the hospital. Darci and his mother met them there. The emergency room doctor checked him and said everything looked normal, but he was told to take a stress test.

Not long after that, Danny began to have chest pains and his blood pressure was high again. Thinking he was having congestive heart failure, he went to the doctor for the stress test. After work the next day, he got into the shower and noticed small, red blotches on his skin. They were everywhere! He knew a land surveyor's worst nightmare was getting Rocky Mountain spotted fever or Lyme disease, and he panicked. "Darci! Come here! I'm in trouble!"

Very pregnant, Darci came as fast as she could, pulled back the shower curtain, and stared at him. He cried, "Look at me! What is this rash?"

She said, "Wait a minute. Did they put something on you for the stress test?"

He still didn't get it. "Yes, they were like suction cups to monitor everything."

"Great! Babe, you have Suction Cup disease!"

They laughed until they cried. After that scare and the doctor's instructions to lose weight, Danny succeeded in losing a little; but it wasn't long before he gained it back and felt more like a failure than before. Then he noticed that one of his breasts was swollen and sore. The doctor thought it was from some trauma, but later Danny learned it was because of his weight. He was getting so obese that his body was producing less and less testosterone. The fat was filling him with estrogen. It explained why he had little desire for sex at all. This was another part of his life that was humiliating.

In all this turmoil and regardless of all their problems, God continued to answer their prayers. Danny and Darci look back and shake their heads in awe and gratitude. They began to pray for enough money so that Darci could quit working and stay home. It wasn't long after that when Danny received another pay increase, and they knew it was God's answer to their prayers.

On January 22, 1999, Charles David Cahill was born as it snowed outside. The doctor had decided to do a C-section. At 340 pounds, Danny could not fit into the surgical uniform. Because he couldn't zip it up, everyone called him Elvis! In the white jumpsuit, he looked just like "The King" in his later years. Nevertheless, witnessing the birth of their son was an amazing experience.

From the beginning David was a good baby, and he was so handsome! He brought Danny and Darci closer together, as they loved and cared for him. They savored every moment with him. He enjoyed his nursery and rarely cried. And thanks to some wonderful people at the church, he had some awesome clothes.

Staying at home with a baby was a blessing, but it was also a challenge. Darci prayed to have a friend on her side of town that she could pray with and do things with, someone who had a child David's age. It wasn't long before she ran into a girl she had known in high school. Jessie had a baby girl about six months younger than David, and they hit it off right away. They did almost everything together, like cleaning, working out, play dates, and grocery shopping. Today, she and Jessie remain great friends and prayer partners.

Meanwhile, God had been dealing with Danny and Darci about using credit cards. They both felt they were to stop using them. The problem was that Danny was spending much of his paycheck at the track, so Darci had little money to buy groceries and other necessities. She was forced to use the credit cards for these things, not really understanding why. Danny was so self-deceived about his gambling, he would get mad at her for using them!

At the same time, it seemed God was showing Darci that she could do without the credit cards again and again. They took a trip to Tulsa to see Danny's cousins and went to the mall. As they cruised around Baby Gap, Darci found a cute pair of striped sweatpants, but they cost $24.00 and she would have to put them on the credit card. Just then she heard the Holy Spirit say, "Trust Me to keep My word and give you the desires of your heart."

In her heart, Darci said, "Okay Lord, I am hearing You say not to charge these pants, and You also say obedience is better than sacrifice. So I will put my desires in Your hands." That was on Friday, and the following Sunday morning her friend Karen gave her some bags of clothes for David. When she got home, the first item she pulled out of the first bag was the same pair of sweatpants she had wanted at Baby Gap!

Darci also wanted a porch swing for their house. While at the store, she almost charged it on the credit card. Again, God told her to trust Him, and a few days later Jessie called to say she had a surprise for her—the very same porch swing! God was teaching Darci and showing Danny that no matter what their circumstances, they could trust Him to provide what they needed. He was especially building trust in Darci, a solid trust in His faithfulness that would hold her up when times were hard.

When their microwave broke, it was a major problem. Little David's bottles would have to be warmed up by running hot water over them. It became a hassle, but they couldn't afford to buy a new microwave. Then a few days later, Danny was sitting on the front porch when the UPS truck drove up. He thought, *I wonder what the neighbors are getting?* The man got out of the truck with a large box and asked Danny to sign for it. Darci's friend Kathy had bought them a microwave and had had it shipped to their house!

It was as though God was orchestrating an army to come to their aid in their time of need, and it wouldn't be the last time.

A New Millennium

Danny and Darci started a young married couples' fellowship group at the church, and they enjoyed friendships with other Christian couples their age. Danny was working hard and was very involved with the music team, and Darci was more and more concerned about his health because of his weight. She prayed he would not develop heart disease, diabetes, or have a stroke.

During Christmas 1999, Danny became ill and his temperature was 104.5 on Christmas morning. He was delirious but refused to go to the doctor. He wanted to see David open his presents on his first Christmas, so he got out of bed to watch and promptly returned to sleep. That night he woke up, walked into the hallway, and fell to his knees in severe pain. Darci rushed him to the hospital, where he was misdiagnosed and sent home with a prescription.

On New Year's Eve, as everyone was looking forward to the new millennium and wondering if Y2K would become the nightmare so many were saying it would become, Danny again fell to his knees in severe pain and Darci took him to the emergency room. Again he was misdiagnosed and sent home with another medicine. The doctor in the emergency room told Darci's mother that if it were up to him, he would admit Danny, but he wasn't the doctor in charge. He then urged Danny to follow up with a pulmonary specialist as soon as possible.

On January 3, Danny went to see the pulmonary specialist who examined him briefly and gravely said, "You need to walk across the street and admit yourself to the hospital immediately. You have pleural effusion, which means your abdomen is filling with fluid and pushing up your lung, which is causing the severe pain you are experiencing." For the next eight days, Danny was in the hospital. They first surgically removed the fluid, and then later that day the doctor came to tell him they found suspicious cells in it, and he might have cancer. He said they had already called an oncologist, which put the entire family in a whirlwind of fear.

Panic set in, and Danny was beside himself. He cried hysterically. Darci and their families were even more worried than before. The next day, however, the doctor told them there was no cancer. Danny felt shell-shocked. After he was released to go home, it took him six months to physically recover from all that had happened to him. He worked mostly at home, which only made it easier for him to gamble online and eat whatever and whenever he wanted.

Despite the total lack of catastrophe predicted by the Y2K prognosticators, the year 2000 had begun in a dark shadow for Danny and Darci. Danny was losing his temper more often than before, and Darci often was startled at these fits of rage over little things, especially something to do with money.

Darci preferred not to dwell on this and continued to enjoy being at home with David, spending time with her friends, and being a part of the church. Later in the year she discovered she was pregnant with their second child, and she and Danny were both thrilled. They already had a boy and prayed for a girl. Soon they found out their prayers had been answered.

In the seventh month of Darci's pregnancy, Danny came home from work and announced, "Hey, I put my resume online and someone actually called me! I have a job interview in Tulsa next week."

What Danny did not know was that Darci and her friend Kathy, who lived in Tulsa, had been praying about this for some time. Darci felt God wanted them there, but she knew God would have to move on Danny's heart to make the move. He was so close to his father and mother. Therefore, when Danny announced that he had an interview in Tulsa, she knew it was God's will, and it was going to happen. Danny jumped at any opportunity to make more money, and it was time to make his own name in the surveying business, apart from his dad.

He and Darci also knew they had been running to their parents instead of each other whenever they had a problem in their marriage. This was causing bad feelings between in-laws. If Darci complained about Danny to her parents, they might hold it against him, and the same happened if Danny complained to his parents about Darci. It was time for them to "leave and cleave" to one another, like the Bible said. They needed to work out their problems themselves.

God always has multiple good reasons for what He does. Danny and Darci never could have guessed what was in store for them in Tulsa. In fact, if they had had any inkling of what they were about to go through, they might have said, "No thanks, Lord," packed their bags, and moved to Alaska!

Digging Out of Debt

"Grandpa, what was the war like?"

"Well son, it was a little bit of hell, a little bit of fun, a little bit of excitement, a little boring at times. It was a little of everything, just like life."

This answer sticks with Danny and Darci to this day, because their lives turned out to be one battle after another. They had to learn how to fight and keep on fighting, how to win, how to rejoice and be thankful — and then how to do it all over again.

With all of us, there is this need to believe we can control our lives. This lie continues to plague us even after we give our lives to Jesus. It's called pride. Like Jacob, we wrestle with God over who will call the shots. Alas, there is no escape for any believer! God loves us too much to leave us the way He found us, in our selfish, proud ways. And that's a good thing, because He will turn our worst nightmares into the greatest joys — if we lose the selfish pride and let Him.

A Geographic Cure?

Danny and Darci went to Tulsa for Danny's interview, and two weeks later he was working there. He lived with his cousins and would go back to Del City to spend time with Darci and David on the weekends. He was also working on their house there. More than a year before, they had begun adding on a kitchen and laundry room, doing the work themselves, and the remodel was still unfinished.

Although very pregnant and taking care of a toddler, with the help of friends and family Darci got their house packed. She visited Danny in Tulsa so they could find a place to live. They were glad to find a rental house that was $250 a month less than most houses its size, and it was exciting to move to a new house and a new town. They didn't like leaving family, friends, and their church family whom they loved, but they didn't have too much time to be sad. Just three weeks after they made the move, on May 14, 2001, Mary Claire arrived.

Mary Claire was a VBAC baby. Darci desperately wanted to deliver her naturally, since they had felt the doctor who delivered David had forced the C-Section on them. The doctor had said David was already ten pounds, but he came out nearly two pounds lighter. When Darci went into labor with Mary on Mother's Day, she worked hard and delivered her 22.5 hours later. It was a tough delivery because Mary outdid her brother, weighing in at 10 pounds 3 ounces! This really proved the first doctor was wrong.

From the moment she entered their lives, everyone knew Mary was larger than life. Like her big brother David, she was an easy, happy baby, hardly ever crying. She would lie in her crib and be happy for a half hour or more, patiently waiting for one of her parents to come get her. Later, she would stand up and call out to them instead of crying. The only time she was really difficult was when she was sick. She would fight taking medicine, and Darci or Danny would have to wrap her in a sheet and force the medicine down her throat. Half the time, she'd spit it out!

When it came to their children, although Darci did most of the work, she and Danny adored them and were together in all things concerning them. David and Mary were like two little shining lights, especially during this very dark time in their lives. Darci had gained a lot of weight with her pregnancy, and this time she didn't lose it. She joined Danny in his eating abandonment and soon showed signs of post-partum depression.

Danny couldn't cope with his own mental state and had nothing to give to Darci. Although he worried about her, he began working even longer hours. He was also still working on the kitchen and laundry room in their house in Del City, and for the next three months he travelled there to finish the work so they could sell the house. The stress was horrible. He now weighed about 370 pounds, and his "fuse" became shorter and shorter.

His spirits were lifted for a short time after their house in Del City sold. The minute they signed the papers, even though they made no money on the sale, Danny felt tremendous relief. However, when he returned to the routine of working at a job he did not enjoy, and working so hard but never getting ahead financially, his depression and anger came to the surface again.

Darci thought Danny was frustrated with his weight, and that's why he got so angry. She also noticed he was getting more and more controlling about their finances. He told her never to open a bill. She was to put all bills and any mail that looked like a bill on his desk. He would take care of it. She was always confused because he worked so hard, even going back to Oklahoma City to do extra work, and still they could barely get by each month. God had blessed him with raises and promotions and now a job in Tulsa that paid much more, and still they barely made ends meet.

Darci did not waste time making new friends and becoming better acquainted with Kathy's group of Christian friends. She needed them because the atmosphere in their home was tense. She was on edge whenever Danny was at home because she never knew what would set him off. It also didn't help that it took them a year to decide on a church. Over the years they had heard Tulsa was the "Disneyland of Christianity," with so many great churches, ministries, and Bible schools. Whatever kind of Christian you were, you could find a church to fit you in Tulsa. Sometimes more is not better; it just confuses the issue!

When they finally settled on a church, they dove in to become involved in a church family again. Their happiest days had been spent together in church. Danny began playing guitar, and Darci auditioned for the vocal team. The worship leader said they would like her to begin rehearsing, but it wasn't time for her to actually minister yet. She decided to "pass" on singing for the time being and volunteered to work with the two- and three-year-olds' Sunday school class.

As the weeks passed, Danny began to "hide out" more and more. He worked hard and served at the church, but the light in him was very dim. He did not want to socialize or go anywhere, and both he and Darci became frustrated with the way the church was being run. The senior pastor seemed to be okay with staff pastors coming and going, as if in a revolving door, during the years they were there. The church paid some musicians and didn't pay others, and they were always having a financial crisis. Darci soon discovered that the children's department was not organized. Nevertheless, they knew that was where God wanted them to be, and so they stayed, served faithfully, and learned from the experience.

After several years, God told them to leave the church they were in and they found another church nearby that not only offered great music and teaching but also was run like a well-oiled machine. They both got involved in the music department, making some more good friends, even while their marriage and home life continued to deteriorate.

One significant thing that happened at the new church was that Danny found a mentor. Orlando was the music minister. He also was a mature, compassionate believer, and their mutual love of music cemented the connection. Although Danny's father had taught him many wise things about life, he wasn't much for talking about his faith, and now he was over one hundred miles away. Danny needed a strong Christian man to help him become the man God created him to be, and Orlando was a not just a gifted musician; he was also a gifted pastor.

Darci had also found a core group of women whom she loved and respected for their faith and their lifestyle, and they loved and supported her. She avoided being at home with Danny as much as possible. He was extremely obese, never wanted to do anything with her, and really showed little interest in her or the children unless it benefited him in some way. Where she used to drink and party with friends, at least now she escaped by spending time with her prayer partners. These women, who prayed for her and mentored her, would soon make a huge difference in their lives.

Darci also went to women's Bible studies. She grappled with being the "godly wife." She did what Danny told her to do. She tried not to complain and cry and to pray instead. She prayed God's will and word, believing that what she was praying would come to pass. The thing was, her prayers were not being answered in the quick and easy way they had been when she and Danny had first come to the Lord. It was hard now. It seemed like her prayers were going up, hitting the ceiling, and crashing back in her face. She was also fighting envy and self-pity. All the women around her had plenty of money and never worried about groceries or clothes. If their car broke down it was no big deal; if Darci's broke down, she was stuck at home.

When Mary was about fourteen months old, Darci began going to a Bible study called "Because of Jesus," which was about the Proverbs 31 woman. This woman was amazing. She was a wife, mother, community servant, and businesswoman. Darci learned that she didn't have to strive to be like this woman; because of Jesus, she already was this woman. His promises were already hers.

Darci thought, *If that's the truth, I certainly am not seeing it! And I don't feel like it at all!* She did not realize that she was consumed with Danny and his behavior. She was completely oblivious to her own desires, needs—and problems. Although she thought she was being spiritual, she was actually looking to God as a heavenly "fixer," and He wasn't fixing anything—Danny, their finances, or their marriage. The truth was, she was in need of fixing as much as Danny, but she was so obsessed with him, God could do little with her.

Spiraling Downward

The tables had turned. Now Danny was the addict and she was the enabler. Like her mother had done with her father over the years, she was keeping the peace and in full denial. Her world revolved around Danny—his moods, his needs, and his instructions (or commands). In actual fact, she was living in fear instead of faith. And, of course, God only moves by faith.

Always merciful, every now and then God would be able to break through and bless them. By this time, Danny's gambling had run up the credit cards to the point that nothing was left after he paid their bills. They had two cars, but one broke down, so Darci became stranded at home. He called to tell her that it would cost $900 to fix the car. She got off the phone and started screaming at God. Somewhere in the yelling, she began to remind Him of the promise in His Word that said she would have more than she needed. Then she read Deuteronomy 28:1-14 out loud and cried, "Okay, You are either a man of Your word or You aren't!" She did not realize that she had gone from fury to faith in a matter of seconds. The words she spoke and read had given her that faith.

An hour later, Danny called. He sounded like he was crying. Darci asked, "What's the matter?"

"Babe, you won't believe this. Dean just came in to tell me how much they appreciated the job I'm doing, and he gave me a $1,000 bonus!" Danny's tears were for more than being able to get Darci's car fixed. He knew God was helping him to support his family even while he was failing to do that in so many ways.

God also provided for Darci and their children through her friends. They would give her money to pay for her lunch or dinner when they went out together. They gave her clothes and other things she needed or wanted. Sometimes, this made her situation worse. She knew this was not God's best way to live. She would feel ashamed for always being on the receiving end.

In June 2003, Danny's father had a breathing attack and nearly died. He was on a ventilator for two weeks, and Danny was unhinged at the thought of losing him. This caused him to re-evaluate their move to Tulsa. He talked to Darci, and they began praying about whether they should return to Oklahoma City. In the end, and as his father recovered, they decided to stay in Tulsa. One main reason was that Danny did not want to leave Orlando, who had become an important part of his life.

The old jealousy of Darci's friends revisited Danny. In his eyes, he was working himself to death while she went out with her friends and spent his hard-earned money. When she told him that her friends were paying for it, he resorted to believing she was having fun while all he did was work. To him, this justified his gambling. After all, he was the one who worked so hard for this money, right? Of course, focusing on her and all her faults was a good escape from facing his own weaknesses. He was a runner. He ran from everything at a breakneck speed like the classic workaholic. He drove back and forth to Oklahoma City to make extra money. Working two jobs caused more stress, and he ate and gambled even more.

One day he woke up at a red light with his foot on the brake. He had fallen asleep at the wheel. For a long time he had had sleep apnea, but now it was life threatening. The doctor put him on a machine that made him sleep like a baby, so Danny was ecstatic. He had more energy than he had had in a long time. However, he had become too heavy to sleep in their bed, so they bought a recliner for the living room, which was where he began to spend the night. Eventually they moved the recliner into the bedroom, so at least they could sleep beside each other.

Obviously, there was little intimacy between Danny and Darci. They were repeating the old pattern from when they were first married, each coping by escaping, leading separate lives, and occasionally coming together for the sake of their children or because something required the attention of both of them. They had become roommates again, miserable ones.

In the spring of 2004, Danny went to a doctor's appointment, and his doctor asked him, "What's wrong today?" That was all it took for Danny to fall apart, sobbing. Consequently, the doctor prescribed anti-depressants. This did make him feel better and some of his anger subsided, but it also made his weight increase to 420 pounds within the first month.

In June, it had been a year since Danny's father had had his breathing attack. He had been diagnosed with Chronic Obstructive Pulmonary Disease (COPD) but was doing a little better. Danny's parents decided to move to an acreage outside Oklahoma City, which was always their dream, so Danny went to help them move. During his last trip from their old house, Danny drove up to a semi-circle of chairs in the driveway. The entire family was waiting for him. They had orchestrated an intervention to pressure him to lose weight. Each one told him how much they loved him, cried over his condition, and begged him to do something about it. His mother said she was afraid he would die before she did. They offered to pay for lap band surgery, anything, to help him get the weight off and get healthy again.

Danny felt ashamed and hurt, but his pride rose up and he told them he would lose the weight by himself. He appreciated their concern. He was concerned too! And he promised to lose weight. Instead, he gained more, and from that time on he fluctuated between 440-460 pounds.

His parents also advised him and Darci to buy a house instead of continuing to rent. They would be investing their monthly payments instead of throwing the money away on rent. Danny said that it wasn't possible with their present debt-to-income ratio, so his parents offered to loan them the money to get out of debt.

Darci had a bad feeling about this, and she was against the idea; but she remained silent.

After finding out Danny and Darci owed $16,700 on their credit cards, Danny's parents fumed! They told him they could never let the credit card companies take his hard earned money. They told him to consider bankruptcy, but in the end they made the loan of $16,700. Danny and Darci agreed to pay them back when they could. From that moment until they paid them back, their relationship was strained.

Because of his parents' financial investment in their future, they felt entitled to comment on every purchase or financial move Danny and Darci made, beginning with the house they chose to buy. His parents said it was too much house for them, but Danny was adamant that it was a great deal. As it turned out, it was, and they are still living in that house as of this writing. However, it required a lot of work, and they ended up spending about $12,000 to improve it initially.

By October, Danny's gambling debts began mounting up again, and things became even tighter than before. Now he not only was juggling all the bills, but an additional $300 a month for the new house payment. The house was bigger and had a pool—and they owned it—so it required more maintenance than the rental had required. The continual weight gain, the lack of connection with Darci, and the mounting debt were like mountains sitting on top of Danny's head. To make matters worse, Orlando announced that he was moving to Houston to pastor another church!

Darci knew that with Orlando gone, Danny might fold. She prayed for him to be strong, and she turned even more to her prayer partner friends for help. Her heart was aching for the person she had married. She felt abandoned by Danny and abandoned by God. She was going to the Bible studies, praying with her friends, serving in church, taking care of her husband and kids, and yet her life was miserable. She knew everything God promised her in His Word, and she was doing everything she was supposed to do, but nothing changed.

She became more and more desperate for God to do something, anything to help Danny lose weight and get his life straightened out. Of course, by that time she was very overweight herself, but all she could see was Danny and his problems. He worked so hard. He served at the church. They gave whenever they could give. Why didn't they ever have any money?

If anyone asked her friends about Darci, they would say, "She's a woman of faith," but she was drowning in fear and confusion.

All Things Hidden Become Known

Some of Darci's prayer partners not only had great faith but great wisdom and discernment. They knew Darci was pretending everything was fine when it wasn't. She would say, "It's all good because I have a good God," when it wasn't good and God had nothing to do with it. Something was terribly wrong, and they knew it.

Darci never wanted to be at home, especially with her husband. She was continually asking for prayer for their finances, and yet she had no idea what "their finances" constituted. Danny had a great job and worked hard, but still they saw how the family suffered. They knew Danny had tight control over Darci's every move. Yes, something was wrong, but would Darci be willing to see it? Her rose-colored glasses were so dense. They prayed for them to be shattered.

One evening Danny came home and noticed that Darci had opened a bank statement for his land surveying company. He flipped out and screamed, "Don't ever open anything that has my name on it. If it isn't addressed to Darci Cahill, it's none of your business!" He didn't realize that Darci's friend was in the room until she quickly said good-bye and left.

Her friend later called and told Darci that she had no idea Danny was treating her that way. Didn't it bother her that he was being verbally abusive to her? And didn't she think it strange that he hid all their financial statements from her?

Having a third person "witness" the life she was leading with Danny cracked Darci's fragile fantasy that everything was okay. Now several other friends began to ask the pointed questions and encouraged her to face facts. They told her that a husband and wife should make all decisions regarding their finances together. They were to be one in all things. Darci knew she and Danny had not felt like they were one in a long, long time!

Finally, one of her prayer partners offered to come over and help Darci sift through all the bank statements, bills, and credit card history. All of her friends would be praying that she would find out the truth and have the courage to confront Danny. What she and her friend found was more staggering than they had guessed. They had no savings. She saw that $300-700 went to online poker every month, and there were other gambling debts as well. She couldn't believe how much they were in debt because of gambling. Danny had another addiction besides food.

When he got home from work, Darci served the family dinner, got the kids to bed, and Danny sat down to watch the World Series. After the Red Sox beat his beloved St. Louis Cardinals, he was going to face something far worse. Darci called from their bedroom, "Babe, we have to talk!" In a few moments he came through the door and his eyes opened wide when he saw what she had found. All their financial records were stacked on the bed.

His secret exposed, Danny looked relieved and said, "It's over. I'm done. It won't happen again." Then he turned away from her to walk out of the room.

"Wait! We need to talk about this. You have—"

He turned his head as he walked out the door. "I told you. It's finished. I'm through gambling." Darci stood there, shaking. She needed to express her anger. She wanted answers or some kind of consolation from him. He didn't even repent or act like he was sorry at all! Obviously, her feelings didn't matter. She was nothing to him. And her trust in him was completely spent.

As far as Danny was concerned, he had acted as a man of action. He would simply not gamble again. It was over. Pride and control were still hanging on tight! Although he could not get the look of betrayal on Darci's face out of his mind, and he knew it would take a miracle to win back her trust, he was certain he could do it. He was in control.

Like all insecure but proud individuals, he became defensive. In the days directly following the confrontation, he tried to convince Darci that the financial situation wasn't that bad. Several times he blamed their exorbitant debt on her credit card usage, which had been a common tactic of his throughout their marriage. He would fly into a rage almost every time Darci used a credit card, no matter what the situation. She would only use them to buy necessities like groceries, food, and clothing. Occasionally she would use them for a dinner with friends or a birthday gift. By the time she confronted Danny with his gambling, she felt trapped in a prison—and Danny was the jailor.

After she had discovered his gambling debts, however, Darci grew bolder. One day she blew up in return and reminded Danny of something that had taken place when they still lived in Del City. Back then, he was blaming her for running up their credit cards, so she had challenged him to "take a good look at who spent what on what." Now Danny secretly took up the challenge. He drew three columns on a piece of paper. One was for his personal charges, one was for Darci's personal charges, and one was for their joint charges for Christmas presents. When he was finished tallying up the total of each column, his heart sank. He had spent almost as much on himself as they had spent on the entire family Christmas, which was hundreds of dollars. Darci's personal column was $64.00.

After this revelation, Danny's urge to gamble subsided, seeing clearly how his addiction had affected their life and relationship. Although Danny promised Darci to stop gambling, he had not admitted his addiction to it, nor had he repented of it. He still had to be in control. Over the next couple of years, there were a few times when he would sneak out to a casino and gamble, mostly when Darci left town and he would only allow himself one hundred dollars to play poker. Sometimes he won; sometimes he lost. But he hid this from Darci, afraid she would freak out at the idea of him in a casino.

Darci wanted to be the submissive, Christian wife, but she was deeply hurt that Danny had just dismissed her when she had confronted him. If her heart had been callous toward him before, now it became cold. She entered a new phase of denial. This time, she became insensitive to the problems he faced because of his weight. She would worry about his health from time to time, but she had no idea that he was in so much pain both physically and emotionally. He had hurt her so much that she disconnected.

Then there was the question: How would they face this mountain of debt? They still believed in a God who loved them and could show them the way. He was still their hope.

Finding the Plan

Danny had spent years hiding credit card and bank statements like a junkie hides drugs, and Darci had spent years working hard to be a great enabler and to stay in complete denial. They had a lot of bad thinking to replace with truth that would set them free in the area of their finances. Their relationship was at an all-time low, but they had to put their hurt and anger aside to deal with the immediate problem of their finances. The first order of business, of course, was how to pay off the gambling debts.

They had about $45,000 in credit card debt. They knew they couldn't ask Danny's parents to bail them out again; they still owed them the $16,700! They talked about bankruptcy, and Darci met with a bankruptcy attorney. The attorney outlined what they would need to do: Stop paying all bills for six months, and shut down Cahill Land Surveying. This was the company his father had founded, and now Danny owned and operated it. It provided the extra income they needed so badly. The attorney also said that the creditors would likely go after the money Danny had paid to his contract worker, which was something Danny could not live with.

Many people were telling them to go ahead and declare bankruptcy, and Darci wanted a "quick fix," but Danny had no peace about going that route. He became adamant that he would pay it off. He said, "I dug this hole, and I have to dig myself out of it." (It was the closest thing Darci got to an apology or any kind of repentance.) However, he agreed to pray that God would give them a sign about which way to go, because in many ways, declaring bankruptcy would be easier.

That Sunday at church, Joyce Meyer was the guest speaker. She looked right at them and said, "I'm going to start you out with a statement: The only way out is through. Some of you have been running from issues that you needed to face for years, and as long as you run from something, it has control over you. If you keep going around the mountain, you're just going to end up with it right there in front of you again. You can't take a shortcut. Shortcuts don't work! You're going through that mountain, and then you will leave it behind for good."

Danny and Darci looked at each other knowingly. They had taken a shortcut by borrowing money from Danny's parents, and now they were in a worse situation. Danny whispered, "That's the word we prayed for," and Darci nodded. They knew God was speaking to them through Joyce. Shortcuts didn't work. They didn't deal with the real problem, which was bad thinking and the bad habits it produced. They needed to change their thinking and their behavior when it came to dealing with money. They needed to go through that mountain and leave it behind.

They went home and cut up their credit cards. By shutting down $60,000 in lines of credit, it ruined their credit score; but they knew this was necessary to stop accruing more debt. They enrolled in a debt reduction program, where the credit card interest rate was frozen at 6 percent and monthly payments were assessed. They attended a financial seminar at church called Financial Peace University and learned the principles of good stewardship and management of personal finances. And, they enlisted the prayers of their friends and family as they made this journey "through the mountain" of debt.

The question arose, "How much should we give to the church?"

They knew all about tithing, or giving a tenth of their income. Giving 10 percent was impossible, however, so they asked the Lord to show them what to give. They read in the Bible that they were to purpose in their hearts what to give to God, and then they were to give joyfully and willingly. After looking at their budget and praying about it, they had peace about giving $25 a week until the debt was paid off and they could give more. At every turn in the following years, God honored their commitment and blessed them often.

Getting through that mountain was harder than they originally thought it would be. A third of Danny's take-home pay went to the debt, and he worked two jobs. When it was reduced by ten thousand, they felt encouraged that their efforts were working, but they had such a long way to go! Finally, the day came when they only owed $15,000. They were tempted to apply less of their income to the debt and have a little more to give to the church and spend on themselves, but they resisted the temptation and stuck with the plan they knew God had given them.

Four and a half years after they began paying off the credit card debt, they made the last payment. It was a time of great celebration and hope for the future. In the meantime, there were other mountains they needed to go through. Yes, life was one battle after another, and there were no shortcuts, but they were determined to lose those mountains and gain new freedom.

Getting Real with God

Every time Danny and Darci faced something that was wrong in their lives, to get truly free of it they had to do two things: get real with each other and get real with God. People say that confession is good for the soul because it is. They felt immeasurable relief when their denial of the gambling problem came to light and that dark secret was exposed. They realized that secrecy was the darkness that gave the habit power over them. Once it came into the light, it lost its hold.

The next step was to dig their way through more than the mountain of debt. In order to lose that mountain and leave it behind for good, they had to dig out the root lies that caused that mountain and replace those lies with the truth. Jesus said that the truth we know is what sets us free, and that knowing is not just an intellectual concept in our heads but a reality in our hearts. Only a deep, intimate knowing of truth could set a course of freedom for their life together.

Danny and Darci found Jesus' words to be right on! Knowing truth is the key to real and lasting peace, and that can only come from getting real with God in a gut-level, often heart-wrenching, brutal honesty. It meant they couldn't blame anyone (even God). They had to take full responsibility for their life: their success or failure, their happiness or unhappiness, and the full gamut of their thoughts, emotions, speech, and behavior.

The irony is that they first had to own it to surrender it. Why is that? Once we take full responsibility, we realize how helpless we are to change ourselves! We need someone greater to do that. That's when we give it all to God. Then our only responsibility is to follow Him so He can do what He does best: turn our mourning into dancing and transform our ashes into something beautiful.

Hard Times

Danny's new obsession was working all the jobs he could work to pay off the debt as soon as possible. His only friend in his martyrdom was food. He believed Darci didn't appreciate what he was going through. From his point of view, she just stayed home and played with the kids all day, and when they entered school, it only allowed her to have more fun with her friends. Darci, on the other hand, was having a harder and harder time at home, especially if one or both of the kids got sick.

One day Danny was hard at work when Darci called. David had been home from school for two days with what they thought was the flu. She was extremely agitated. "I'm taking David to the doctor now! Something is wrong, and I think you need to meet us there." Danny rushed to the doctor's office and went into shock when he saw his precious eight-year-old son. His lips had turned black and were inside out, and he writhed in pain. Fear gripped all of them when the doctor ordered them to immediately take David to Saint Francis Children's Hospital, where he was admitted and initially misdiagnosed with herpes.

After three days of extreme pain, an infectious disease specialist examined David and made the correct diagnosis. He had Stevens-Johnson Syndrome. Here is what the Mayo Clinic says about this condition on their website:

> Stevens-Johnson syndrome is a rare, serious disorder in which your skin and mucous membranes react severely to a medication or infection. Often, Stevens-Johnson syndrome begins with flu-like symptoms, followed by a painful red or purplish rash that spreads and blisters, eventually causing the top layer of your skin to die and shed.

Just one year before, another child had been admitted to that hospital with this same problem, so the specialist and the staff were familiar with it. Danny and Darci saw God's hand in that! About three hundred new cases are diagnosed in the United States each year, so the condition is not very well known. Nevertheless, it is one of the most painful skin diseases a human being can endure, and some die if it is not caught in time.

Danny's fear turned into sheer rage that God would allow his child to go through such a horrifyingly painful trial. He knew God had not caused the disease, but he blamed Him anyway. No child should have to go through this! At one point, Danny shook his fist at God and told Him to go to hell. Darci was equally upset. After all, they were doing everything they were supposed to do! They had faced the gambling problem. Danny was working two and sometimes three jobs to get out of debt. They were going to church and serving in the ministry. And yet God just sat back and watched while this insidious disease tried to burn up their son from the inside out!

Church members and family gathered around Danny and Darci to pray and help them with whatever they needed. Darci stayed by David's side, trying to remain strong for her suffering child but feeling helpless. She was questioning God's faithfulness. Then Danny had to tear himself away on the second day because he became terribly sick himself. He went home and, despite the doctor's advice, looked up the disease on the Internet. What he read scared him even more. Two days later he went back to the hospital, and David was much worse.

When the doctor told them they should prepare for the worst, Darci had to leave the room. She went into the hall and cried aloud, "Okay Lord, are You a liar? You said if we prayed and believed, You would heal. This little boy is crying out to You, trusting You. I want to know. Are You going to come through for him?!"

At one point David had cried out to Danny and Darci, "Pray for me!" Danny was so mad at God that his little boy's faith rocked him, and then it humbled him. He thought, *Whatever Darci and I have done wrong, at least our son trusts God. We must be doing something right.* He realized that this wasn't about him! It was about David. God had a plan for David's life too, and the enemy was trying to take him out before he could even understand what his purpose was.

Now Darci was crying out to God, and all she heard was, "Read Matthew 7:9. "She looked it up in her Bible, and it said, "Which of you, if your son asks for bread, will give him a stone?"

She closed her Bible. "Okay, Lord."

The doctors explained that David's case was critical. There was a procedure that might work, but it was dangerous. It would likely cure him if it didn't kill him, and they believed it was the best alternative they had at this point. Danny and Darci felt it was what should be done, even in the midst of horrible fears, and so the doctors did an immunoglobulin transfusion.

Almost immediately, David began to get better. Seven days later he went home, and three weeks after that he went back to school. However, it would take him about six months to get back to his normal self. As for his parents, Danny and Darci were exhausted even in their relief; both of them had been shaken in their faith.

Toward the end of David's hospital stay, the doctors had sent Danny home because he had become so ill. Later, he had another stress test because he was having blood pressure problems and thought he was experiencing heart palpitations. The stress test came back negative, but he insisted something was wrong and began wearing a heart monitor. The doctor said he was having anxiety attacks, which became more controllable after he was put on a different anti-depressant. Still, at 460 pounds, his weight was at an all-time high.

One day Danny and Darci were having lunch at a restaurant, which was always dangerous because Danny was so heavy he could break a chair. In fact, this had happened several times and was horribly embarrassing. He saw an extremely overweight man get up and watched him walk out. The man was so heavy that he felt sorry for him. He pointed him out to Darci and asked, "How big am I compared to that guy?"

Darci had a stricken look on her face. "Babe, you're much bigger."

Danny was mortified. To a certain degree he had been able to deny just how overweight he had become, but not now.

He developed several infections in his calves, which were hot to the touch. The doctor put him on powerful antibiotics to break up the infections. Once, while he was lying in his recliner, he looked down at his leg and saw a stream of liquid coming out of a sore. The edema was so bad, his legs felt like tree stumps leaking sap. This was an initial sign of congestive heart failure, which added to his fears.

Now Danny felt hideous. Whenever he looked at himself in the mirror, he saw a monster, not a man. He was so wrapped up in himself and his problems that he assumed his wife was leading the perfect life—and he made no attempt to discover the truth. He would pout or complain when she went out with her friends. After all, he never had fun. He spent all of his time working! He would tell her he was doing all the work and she was just spending the money. When she would tell him that her friends were paying for it, that reminded him that he was the reason they were in this financial mess. Then he would get defensive and try to find fault with her elsewhere.

The Real Sickness

Some Christians live terribly dysfunctional lives. Many are bound in addictions and co-dependency, like Danny and Darci. Many avoid the parts in the Bible that challenge them to grow up and learn the practical wisdom to live life well and get along with people. And then others just get their ticket to heaven and continue to live the way they want to live. None of this is what Jesus had in mind when he died on the cross!

Danny and Darci both loved Jesus. Tears came to their eyes every time they thought about Him taking all the beatings, the whipping, the rejection, being spit upon, being separated from the Father, and dying for their sins. Their hearts melted when they realized He did all this because He loved them and wanted them to be with Him forever. What they had not come to grips with was that He also wanted them to be free to be themselves and accomplish what they were supposed to accomplish in life.

Because of this lack of understanding, they had a distorted concept of unconditional love. They thought they had to prove their love, and that meant self-sacrifice: sacrifice of their dreams, ambitions, and even their spiritual health. As a result, they turned agape love into self-pity and a false martyrdom. Danny had to "lay down his life" for his family by doing a job he wasn't passionate about; Darci had to "lay down her life" for Danny and her children by completely ignoring her own needs. They were convinced they were doing this out of unconditional love!

This kind of "sacrificial love" came easy to both of them. Danny had been there year after year, working with his father, believing that only a steady job and working long hours would make him a good husband and father. Darci had watched her mother endure and ignore her father's behavior for years. Of course, what they learned from their parents wasn't all bad, but they also mistook misery and joylessness to be a major part of the Christian life as soon as tough times arrived. In the first years of their journey of faith, they had found a new intimacy and understanding, but then the following years of secrecy and "busyness" seemed to have killed the intimacy and brought back confusion, distrust, and even bitterness. There was a severe disconnect between them.

Darci was shaken to her core not only by Danny's gambling addiction, but by his refusal to even talk to her about it. Moreover, his lack of remorse and repentance were things she could not forgive. She became bitter and her heart turned hard toward him. She hated his obesity. She despised their lack of intimacy and his unwillingness to communicate anything but negativity. And she resented the fact that the household had always and still remained centered around him. She felt that she and the children were simply there to meet his needs. She slowly came to the point where she hated to be home.

But these were not "Christian" character traits or thinking! So she could not admit them. She was in such denial that most of the time she had no idea she really felt this way. Therefore, her emotional pain caused a distortion of the truth. The truth was that their family life did revolve around Danny and his needs, but Danny was extremely sick, and she missed that part.

Darci was so consumed with her own pain that she could not even sense Danny's. She didn't want to sense it because her own pain was already too much for her to bear—and she proudly bore it by herself. In her eyes, she loved Danny unconditionally like a good saint should, praying fervently for him day and night!

When bitterness takes hold of a Christian's life, that believer is more miserable than when the same thing happens to an unbeliever. An unbeliever doesn't know there is another way to live. A child of God does. Darci had experienced the joy and freedom of forgiving and being forgiven. She knew how awesome it was to live fully for God and not for herself. She also knew the joy of loving others when they didn't love her or act like they loved her, a joy based solely on her relationship with God and no one else. But these truths had become twisted by her emotional pain, and she began living a lie.

She believed that because she still went to church, served in the music ministry, was a part of a women's prayer group, and attended a women's Bible study, she was living like a free, forgiven and forgiving child of God. The truth was, she was playing religious games to get what she thought she wanted. She was hurt and wouldn't go to the Doctor. And the irony was that she couldn't admit she was hurt because she had to be a spiritual wonder woman.

Undergirding her denial was that all this time, the spiritual gifts God had given Darci continued to help others. She could powerfully pray for people and prophesy over them—and good things would happen. Her friends were still a priority, and she helped several in their marriage problems. She supported another when her baby died of SIDS. She had to tell one friend that her husband was cheating on her, but then held her hand and encouraged her as God completely restored their marriage. Any energy she had went into helping others. This proved to her and the Christian world that she was okay—and enabled her to avoid herself.

Ministering to others, however, also fueled her depression. She saw only the tragedy and heartache. Her heart began to cry out, "Why did David, our sweet little boy, have to go through such pain and suffering? Why did my friend's baby die, God? Why are so many of our good friends having terrible marriage problems? Why did our friend, a young mother of children, die of cancer? Why did my other young friend just drop dead one day? Your Bible is filled with promises to us of an abundant life, and after years of struggle, Danny and I still can barely make ends meet! Just who are You, God, anyway?"

And then there was Danny. What had happened to him? Had God even noticed his weight, his temper, how he treated her and the kids? Her faith and trust weakened as she looked to the God who had saved her and initially healed her marriage, yet now seemed to be far away and totally uncaring. Her core beliefs were severely shaken.

Darci was able to keep busy enough to ignore her inner life and all of her doubts and fears for a while. She had no idea what was really going on in her home and with her husband because she wasn't hearing God for her life. She wasn't communing with Him and learning from Him for herself. She was "working" Him and expecting Him to fix everything and everyone around her to meet her expectations and give her a good life. From time to time a marriage was restored or someone, like David, was healed. But for the most part, God was not doing what she truly wanted.

For years, Darci had worried and wondered about their finances. She had prayed and prayed for God to give them a breakthrough. She never thought the breakthrough would be uncovering Danny's gambling addiction and all the debts he had incurred! And then he brushed her off! Now they were chipping away at the debts, but they still had no money for anything extra each month. Danny still lost his temper frequently and put her and the kids on edge. He never wanted to go anywhere or do anything. All this was a constant reminder of his deceit and then his rejection of her.

Then there was his weight, which had reached an all-time high of 460 pounds. What kind of husband and father lets himself go like this? He only got up when he had to, which meant that she did just about everything for him. He slept in the recliner by their bed, and on the rare occasions that Darci initiated making love, it was difficult, to say the least. He, of course, had lost all interest in sex. She took this to mean he had lost all interest in her. In fact, the lack of testosterone and over-abundance of estrogen had completely taken away his sex drive. This was something they would learn later. In the meantime, she felt even more rejected, unloved, and ugly.

Her beliefs were justified whenever she looked in the mirror. Darci had gained an exorbitant amount of weight herself. However, at least she was still active. She got up in the morning. She got the kids up and to school. She then fell on the couch and slept until she had to get up to get the kids, fix dinner, and get them to bed. The next day she would do the same thing unless there was a Bible study or prayer meeting to go to. In essence, she was floating through the days, sleeping whenever she didn't have to do something else. She didn't enjoy much of anything about her life.

She would see people at church and smile brightly when they asked, "Hey Darci! How're you doin'?"

"It's all good! We serve a good God!"

Before David had gotten sick, she often questioned the goodness of God. Now that he had recovered, Darci had no more strength to go to church. It was a charade she just couldn't keep up anymore, and it wasn't helping. Danny got disappointed, then angry when he had to get the kids and go by himself, but her depression had become so severe that she didn't care. It was if she was in a deep, dark hole. She was screaming and no one could hear her. She felt alone, crazy, and unstable.

Did God turn away from Darci in disgust? No! He already knew this was going to happen to her and to many of us. In His mercy, He created our bodies to react when we aren't living according to His truth. For example, if you eat good food your body will remain healthy, but if you habitually eat junk food and too much of it, your body will become sick. Moreover, if you are deeply hurt or offended and you forgive, your body will relax and remain healthy; if you refuse to forgive and turn bitter, over time your body will break down. He built this into us so that we would know when something was wrong in our lives.

God knew exactly what would get Darci back on track.

A Very Bad Hair Day

There is a verse in the Bible about a woman's hair. First Corinthians 11:15 says, "If a woman has long hair, it is her glory." Maybe that is why women are so sensitive about their hair—having a bad hair day means her life is not so glorious!

One Friday night, the whole family was in Danny and Darci's bedroom watching a movie. Danny had fallen asleep in his recliner and the kids were asleep on the bed when Darci's head started itching. She went into the bathroom and began brushing her hair. She glanced down and noticed that hair was falling into the sink. Completely stunned, she kept brushing and the hair kept falling out. She tried to wake up Danny, but he was in a deep sleep and didn't respond, so she gave up and sat on the bed in shock.

She called her friend Tammie and told her what was happening, but Tammie reassured her it was probably nothing. Every woman's hair fell out now and then. A few weeks later, when the two of them were Christmas shopping, her attitude changed. Darci bent down to pick something up in a store and Tammie saw a huge bald spot on the top of Darci's head. "Darci, this is crazy! You need to see a doctor." They guessed it had something to do with all the stress of David's illness, which had occurred earlier that year.

Danny noticed there was much more hair around the shower drain. He was constantly picking up a handful and throwing it away. Then the drain became so clogged that he had to get a plumber's snake to unclog it. He pulled out clumps of hair from the pipe. When he examined Darci's head, he saw more than one bald spot, which scared him. They wondered if she had a disease of some kind.

In December 2007 Darci went to the doctor, and in the weeks to come it seemed he gave her every test known to the medical profession. By the end of January, none of the tests revealed any problems. Finally, Darci sat in his office and the doctor asked her, "Are you stressed about anything?"

Without hesitation she answered, "No, I don't think I have anything to be stressed about."

The next time she was with her friends, Darci broke down, crying about Danny's weight and their finances. She had broken down with them before; in fact, more often than she could admit. Now she let everything spill out. Danny was obese and angry all the time. She had freaked out in front of her kids a couple of times. At one point, she told Danny she felt like "pulling a Marie Osmond," who had recently gotten in her car and driven away from her home in a deep depression. Too often, that sounded like a great idea! It seemed like nothing God promised her was manifesting in her life, and she hated being at home.

Darci's friends laid it on the line, saying, "This is ridiculous. You have got to get your focus off Danny and onto you and your health, mentally and physically." They told her to eat better and exercise. One offered to pay for counseling sessions. They wrote all their recommendations down and made her sign it, like a contract, and then they all signed it as a show of their support to help her do it.

For the first time in a long time, Darci felt a small glimmer of hope. Then someone asked Darci if she had seen this television show called *The Biggest Loser*. Everyone chimed in, "Yeah! They help obese people lose weight, and it really changes their lives." Then one of them asked, "Why don't we pray that Danny will want to go on the show and that it will change his life?" They all agreed.

Shortly after that, Darci began seeing a counselor, and in February, she decided to attend a personal development seminar in Dallas, which had helped Danny's cousin and his wife change their lives in a radically positive way. They had gone from being on the verge of divorce to acting like newlyweds again. They had a new respect and ability to communicate that Darci envied. Their whole family dynamic had changed for the better, and she wanted that in her own home.

The program involved three weekends, each weekend a month apart. That would mean Darci would be away from home for one weekend in February, one in March, and one in April. Danny had been glad she had started going to counseling (especially since he didn't have to pay for it), and he was willing for her to be gone those three weekends if it would help her. As it turned out, she got a scholarship to go, so all he had to pay for were her travel, food, and hotel. He was worried about her. Between her hair falling out, sleeping most of the day, and not going to church, she needed help. And he was scared. When she started talking about pulling a Marie Osmond, he was afraid she would leave him or worse, commit suicide.

Discovery Time

Darci was packing and getting ready to go to the first weekend of the program in Dallas. David and Mary were in her bed. They had always been good sleepers and stayed in their beds all night, but in the past year, more and more, they were climbing into bed with her. Danny always slept in the recliner by the bed, both because of his inability to lie flat on his back and his severe sleep apnea. Mary looked at her and asked, "Mommy, you're gonna come home, aren't you?"

Darci's heart broke. She wondered if they had heard her talking to her friends on the phone, threatening to leave, to just drive away and never come back. She thought about the fact that they never went anywhere anymore, and the only time the kids had been without her in years was her annual weekend of shopping in Dallas with her mother, sister, and grandmothers.

Darci hugged her and David, whose face was also filled with concern. Then she had to finish packing and say goodbye. Danny was a little put out that she was leaving him with the kids all weekend, and that he couldn't get any work done. All the way to Dallas she cried out, "God, you've got to do something!"

The first weekend in Dallas began the process of opening Darci's eyes to a whole new way of living her life. She set some healthy boundaries and decided to take care of herself. She realized that if she wasn't in good shape, she couldn't be much use to anyone else. The most significant change, however, happened in her relationship with God. She felt like she met the real Jesus for the first time. Instead of doing nothing but petition Him for her friends and family, she began to talk to Him about herself. She let Him in. She unloaded. She screamed and cried and threw a fit—and He was still there, even holding her in His arms. She got real, and He could finally show her what was really going on inside her.

She realized He loved her no matter what—even weighing 239 pounds (ironically the amount of weight Danny would lose on *The Biggest Loser*). She knew He wasn't going anywhere. And although she still didn't fully understand why so many terrible things had happened to people she loved and were living "great Christian lives," she knew one thing for certain: He was the Savior not the destroyer. He and her Father in Heaven wanted the best for her and for everyone. As she experienced wave after wave of Their love, the depression lost its hold on her.

Then it was time to go home—and face Danny.

On the drive home, she cried. "God, help me! I don't know what to do about Danny. I can't change him, no matter how hard I try or what I do. I can't criticize him because I'm so overweight. So I lose thirty pounds, but it has no effect on him! I get all the junk food out of the house and change our diet, and it's like it motivates him to eat more junk! Nothing makes any difference to him! What am I doing wrong? What am I supposed to do? Come on, Lord, throw me a bone or something!"

He answered gently, "Don't do anything. Just give him to Me."

Upon hearing those words Darci physically felt a huge weight being lifted from her shoulders. She finally "heard" what her friends had been telling her for months, maybe years. She needed to get her eyes off Danny and get her own life together.

She also heard God say, "This isn't about you losing weight. I don't want you to subtract. I want you to add to yourself. Be good to yourself."

She said, "All right, Lord, but You're going to have to show me what that means." In the next few weeks, she felt like she should take vitamins. Her body was so depleted, the addition of vitamins made her feel better immediately. She started drinking a lot more water as well. By the time she left for the second weekend, she had lost 22 pounds; and she hadn't even been trying. She also liked getting her nails done, so she started doing that regularly—and what a difference it made!

As she attended the other two weekends, her relationship with the Lord was flourishing. She could hear Him again. Her hair stopped falling out. She had more and more energy to do all the things she needed to do—and new things she wanted to do. By May of 2008, she felt reborn. Danny was still miserable, but now she simply thanked God for helping him and prayed for God's will to be done in his life, that He would give Danny the desires of his heart and bless him in everything he did.

Because Darci's prayer partners had made a pact to pray that Danny would want to get on *The Biggest Loser*, she had started watching the show. One day Danny was walking through the living room when she and Mary were watching it (while eating a huge bowl of ice cream!). He stopped and said, "What the heck are you watching?" He thought the show made fun of obese people, and he stomped out of the room. The following week when the show was on again, he sat down and watched part of it with Darci. The teams were going through a challenge, and Danny turned to her and said, "Man, I am athletic for a guy my size. I think I could do that! I played football, and I think I would be good on that show! And you know what? I haven't felt challenged in years. That's what I need; a challenge!" He got up and left, but Darci thought, *Here we go.*

Shortly before this happened, while she was at a prayer meeting, a new girl had come up to her and prophesied: "There's getting ready to be an event in your life, and God is going to change everything. He's going to bless you beyond measure. The blessings are going to come so quickly, it will overwhelm you." When Danny showed an interest in *The Biggest Loser*, she knew that the "new girl" was speaking God's truth.

To help pay off their debts, Darci had taken a job working as a court liaison for supervised visits between children and their parents. It was extremely stressful and Danny was worried some irate father or mother would try to hurt Darci for just doing her job. He urged her to quit, and she did. She began cleaning houses again, but she was having allergic reactions to some of the cleaning agents. This made Danny feel guilty, but he knew they needed the money. Finally, God tapped Darci on the shoulder and said, "It's time to clean and organize your own house." She began to take pride in her home again.

There was no question that Darci was transformed. Just after the first weekend seminar, David and Mary said, "We want Mom to go back. She's a better mom now! She doesn't yell as much and is happier." Darci urged Danny to go, but he said, "I appreciate that you want me to go…and perhaps I will when times get better… but I am fine…I don't need it and we don't have the money."

Many of their friends began going to the seminars, and then Kathy asked her husband to go. Her husband asked Danny one day, "What do I do? Go to this stupid thing and come back to Kathy and lie about liking it?"

Danny answered, "No. You go because she wants you to go and she is important to you, and if you don't like it you just tell her it's not for you and don't go back. Just tell her the truth." This was ironic, because Darci had been begging Danny to go for months, and he wouldn't. But here he was, convincing his friend to go anyway! After his friend returned from the program, Danny could not believe the change in the man, who then offered to pay for Danny's first weekend. Now money was no longer an excuse, and he felt he had to go, so his first weekend was in June.

When Danny was gone, Darci was laying in bed with Mary Claire, watching a movie. They began talking, and Darci felt she needed to reassure her. "Mary, you never have to worry. I will always be with Daddy, and I will always be here with you and David." Mary began shaking and crying. Obviously, she had been scared her family was going to fall apart like other families had. Then she suddenly relaxed like she hadn't in years. Darci knew then just how much their turmoil had been affecting the children.

At the seminar, Danny was doing okay until there was an exercise, where each person had to be physically held up by the other attendees. When Danny saw them holding the first person, he wanted to disappear. He went from person to person, saying, "You don't have to hold me up. It's okay. We can skip me."

The head of the seminar cried confidently, "Are you crazy? We can hold you up, buddy!" They held him up while they played a song that said you can always start again tomorrow. This experience had a profound effect on Danny. It showed him there was no shame in getting help. He didn't have to do everything by himself. He didn't have to control everything. And no matter how big his problem, there were others who could, and would, help him.

For the first time he also saw how he had been treating his family. He was losing his temper and not considering their feelings or desires because he was so wrapped up in himself and his daily struggle. Instead of asking for help, he had to prove he could do everything on his own. As a result, instead of coming home to love and nurture his family, he blamed them for all the work he had to do. He took everything out on them.

He came home from the seminar wanting to be a different husband and father, but he found that it was hard work! He knew he had a long way to go, but he was encouraged when David and Mary said he was a better dad and was yelling a lot less! Darci told him she felt like the joyful, passionate man she had fallen in love with was back. That gave him the determination to do the other two weekends.

At his second weekend, in July, Danny wrote in his journal:

What to do to achieve my dreams:

1. Live my contract: "I am a joyful and passionate man!"

2. Lose the weight!

3. Lose the debt

(2 & 3 can be achieved by winning *the Biggest Loser!*)

[signed] Charles D. Cahill

July 19, 2008

By the end of that weekend, he had declared to everyone, "I'm going to get on that show and win it! I believe it is my destiny." When Danny got home, he shared his decision to get on *The Biggest Loser* with Darci, who was thrilled and so thankful to God. She could hardly believe she had ever doubted Him or His goodness.

The next time she met with her prayer group, Darci broke the good news that Danny was going to try to get on *The Biggest Loser*. The same "new girl" said, "He's going to win that show. He won't get on the first time he tries, but he's going to win it when he does." She would prove to be speaking for God again. The rest is history for anyone who watched *The Biggest Loser*, Season 8.

Interestingly enough, in the Bible the number eight symbolizes new beginnings.

Pressing In to Win

After Danny and Darci had both given their lives to Jesus and become involved in the church, God managed to deal with smoking, drinking, and then gambling. He also gave them two beautiful and gifted children. Those who truly love their children will do anything to see them succeed and be happy in life—even deal with their own areas of weakness. Danny and Darci's motivation and resolve to do just that were cemented in a moment of horror concerning their daughter.

Mary Claire walked up to her daddy, threw her arms around his waist, and declared, "Daddy, you're my hero! I want to be just like you."

Danny and Darci beamed with pride and joy that their child loved and respected her father so much that she wanted to be just like him. Then she went on to say, "I want to have a belly just like yours."

That's when the floor seemed to disappear underneath them. At that moment, her daddy had a 69-inch waist.

The Wait

Danny's bulldog commitment to change or die came from that haunting memory of Mary saying, "I want to have a belly just like yours." That was it! There was no turning back. His heart turned toward one goal: Get on *The Biggest Loser*. Danny and Darci would both soon realize that all the years they had spent forcing themselves to stay within a budget, paying their bills on time, and spending wisely—all to get out of debt—had not been punishment. God had been teaching them discipline and perseverance, the discipline and perseverance they had to have to get through the months ahead and learn a better way to live.

They had already figured out that they could not make each other do what was right for them. They could only do what was right for themselves. They had to trust God to lead the other person. The days of controlling and manipulating one another to get their own way, or blaming each other for their problems, were over. It was time to take responsibility for their own success and happiness.

If Danny wanted to be happy and healthy, it was between him and God.

If Darci wanted to be happy and healthy, it was between her and God.

What they could do for each other was pray, ask for help when they needed it, challenge one another, encourage one another, and stay in an attitude of forgiveness, love, and respect. Darci, especially, needed this new understanding to not give up as Danny struggled to get on *The Biggest Loser*.

When they had watched the show the second time together, Danny had said he could do it. Just then Alison Sweeney said, "If you think you have what it takes to be a contestant on *The Biggest Loser*, go to NBC.com and download an application." Darci turned to Danny and said, "Then maybe you should try out." He downloaded the application and printed it, but he didn't fill it out.

The next week they watched the show together again, and Danny said the same things. This time he seemed frustrated and complained that some of the contestants didn't seem to be giving it their all. Darci felt she should challenge him. "You have the application. Are you going to fill it out?"

He filled it out, but there was only one week left to submit it. He hurriedly made a video and sent everything to the given address. He hoped he would be accepted for Season 6, but he wasn't very confident that he would be. As it turned out, he heard nothing. Soon he found out Season 6 had been cast, and he set his sights on Season 7. He tried out with his sister Charla.

One day, Danny heard *The Biggest Loser* was having a casting call in Oklahoma City for Season 7. He took off work, drove down, and went with Charla. They stood in line for hours before they finally sat down for the interview. They felt it went really well. A few days later, they were called back for a second interview, and

Danny felt like the whole process had become surreal. He knew they did well. He wondered if this was it.

People from the show called several times and asked for more information from Danny. He tried out with his friend Will, the bass player from his old church. He also tried out with his friend Ansy, who presently played saxophone in the church band with him. Then he was asked if there were any other family members who could try out with him. That let him know they might be interested. He begged some other family members to try out with him, but they were all too embarrassed to take their shirts off in front of millions of people. He was frustrated. Finally, he and Darci made a video and applied together.

They were so excited when they received word of the deadline for them to hear if he and Charla had been cast for the show. That day came and went, but there was no phone call. Danny was devastated. For a while, he stopped watching the show and would have nothing to do with it.

Darci went to her next prayer meeting totally disheartened. Her friends reminded her that God did things in His timing, not necessarily hers or Danny's. Then her friend Michelle told her that she had met Dan and Jackie Evans from Season 5 at a local news show. Michelle had told the Evans about Danny getting so close to the final auditions. Dan told Michelle that he had tried out more than once before he got on the show and that Danny shouldn't quit. Darci went home and told Danny this, but he was resigned to not try out again.

Danny went back to focusing hard on paying off the debt (he didn't even want to think about how long it was taking). However, he "friended" on Facebook one of the casting people for *The Biggest Loser*. They had a few short conversations and exchanged messages, and eventually Danny's anger subsided and he began watching the show again. He thought Season 7 was excellent.

Then an old friend tagged him with a photo on Facebook. In the picture Danny was seventeen years old, in great shape, wearing a muscle shirt, playing in a band. He turned away and saw a framed picture of golf clubs on his wall. Under the picture was the caption: "Delight yourself in the Lord, and He shall give you the desires of your heart." He loved to play golf. Even at 460 pounds he could golf in the eighties. But golf was not the desire of his heart. He wanted to be healthy and live for his family. He also wanted to perform on stage in front of people again.

He showed the picture of himself at seventeen to his friend and co-worker Glenn and asked, "Why am I not playing music and performing? Why am I sitting here in this office and doing something I never really wanted to do, something I settled for? Why am I here?"

Glenn answered, "I think you are the only one who can answer that. Why are you?"

It hit him like a ton of bricks! The answer to all these desires was to win *The Biggest Loser*. He posted a comment on the photo on Facebook, "I want that body back! I'm trying out for *The Biggest Loser* again!"

Danny went home and printed another application. Then he made several copies. No matter how many times it took, he was going to get on that show. He sent in another video, and then there was another casting call in Oklahoma City. This time it said you could come with or without a partner. He told Darci, "This is it! Last time I think my problem might have been my partners, but this is a singles season. I'm going to do this thing!"

He went to Oklahoma City and got a VIP pass, moving him to the front of the line. He walked in to the interview and sat at a table with other applicants. The interviewer explained, "We've got almost a thousand people today, so time is short. You've got sixty seconds to show me who you are. Make me remember you."

Danny thought the first person was boring. The second one was dull. The third seemed almost crazy. Then it was his turn. He knew he had to be BIG, in more ways than his size! He slammed his hand on the table and as loud as he could he yelled, "Hi! I'm Danny Cahill, and I am the next Biggest Loser! In fact, when you put me on the show, you're going to have cast the Biggest Loser EVER. I have absolutely no doubt that I will lose over 200 pounds! I was born for this!" He went on for over two minutes, and no one could stop him. He realized the people at the other table had stopped talking and were looking at him.

He knew he only had a few seconds left to say something that would do more than shock them by his volume. So out it came: "And I'm tired of being on bottom! I want to be on top again!" Everyone, including the other hopefuls, burst out laughing. They all knew the double meaning. He could mean he was tired of being on the bottom of life, but he could also be saying he was tired of being on the bottom during sex with his wife. Either way, they didn't forget him!

Danny knew he had done what was necessary to make them remember him. To celebrate, he met Darci and her family for ribs and a beer. He told them, "There is no way I am not getting an interview. If they don't remember me, something's seriously wrong!"

Danny got his second interview. As he drove down to Oklahoma City, he knew crying would be effective, so he tried to think of the most heart-breaking things that would make him cry. He finally squeezed out one tear! This was going to be tough!

He arrived and sat on the couch in the lobby. The interviewers came out of the elevator, but they weren't there to get him. They were there to eat breakfast. Danny had arrived 45 minutes early! He watched them eat out of the corner of his eye, trying not to be obvious, which is impossible for a 460-pound man!

The two interviewers went back upstairs, then they returned to get him. They then began the interview. Inside, Danny was screaming, "I gotta cry!" But nothing moved him.

Then he was asked how his weight had affected his life.

In a split second he thought of the physical pain and fear of disease and death. He thought of his inability to be the husband and father he knew he could be. He thought of the embarrassment, the shame, the hurt, the anger, and the depression he had endured all these years. He thought of the disappointment to everyone around him, most of all himself. And he burst into tears. Throughout the interview, the tears seldom stopped. He cried all the way home. As he cried, he saw how much had been bottled up inside him for so long. For such an outgoing, expressive person, his pride had not allowed him to hurt and reach out for help. He had to be the guy who had it all together. Then he laughed. No matter how he tried to hide it, it was so obvious he was the guy who didn't have it all together!

Darci and the kids were so excited, and everyone was praying and believing the time was right. Over the next few months, he was inundated with phone calls and requests. It was taking up so much of their time, and it actually became annoying. They wondered if they were being tested to see if they were really serious. After all, if they picked Danny, they both knew the whole family would be affected. He would have to drop everything to do this, and they would have to support him in it.

It was the end of April 2009. Danny and Darci had just refinanced their home and were driving to the bank to pay their last credit card payment! They hadn't heard anything lately from the casting department of the show. They were trying to trust God, but they were still frustrated. One day at work, Danny looked at the golf picture again and began to weep. He had a fear in the pit of his stomach that he hadn't made it again. He prayed, "God, why do You do this to me? You gave me this desire and now You put me through this dissapointment? You say You aren't a liar, that Your word is true. Then why are You doing this to me?"

He felt like he should read his Bible, so he took it out and placed it on his desk. It seemed to open naturally to Genesis 50:20: "You intended to harm me, but God intended it for good to accomplish what is now being done, the saving of many lives" (NIV).He began to cry and called Darci. She thought he had been fired, because they had been laying off people at his company. Then he said, "I'm going to the show!"

She asked breathlessly, "They called?"

He answered, "No!"

She then asked, "What are you talking about?"

"God told me!"

Darci asked, "What do you mean God told you?"

He read what God had just said to him from the Bible and said, "I believe my being on that show is going to change millions of lives."

She answered, "I believe it too."

And so they continued to wait, but they didn't have to wait long. A few days later, Danny received a call at his office. "Danny, I have some bad news for you." Danny braced himself for the worst. "You're going to have to be away from your family for a week because you are coming to Los Angeles!"

Danny yelled to his co-workers and then called Darci to give her the good news. He put in for the vacation time. When he got home, he read an e-mail that told him what he needed to bring. Darci took him shopping for clothes, and his mother offered to buy him something nice to wear for the trip. Normally, he hated shopping. It was always depressing, and there was little choice in his size, but they did the best they could. They shot video all week. Meanwhile he geared up for a very stressful time, because he knew he would be competing for a spot on Season 8.

The plane ride to Los Angeles was uneventful but embarrassing. They had to buy two seats for Danny, and he had to use the seat belt extender. When he arrived, he got his three bags and went to the shuttle he was to take to Parking Lot C. As he climbed in, he said, "I got more luggage than a woman."

"Watch it, buddy!" a large woman replied with a laugh.

He liked her immediately, and she had a country accent too. Then he noticed as she opened her notebook that the sheet inside had *The Biggest Loser* symbol on it. He panicked. He was worried that he wasn't supposed to talk to any of the other possible contestants, so he turned away and began to ignore her.

After they got off the shuttle she said, "Are you here for the—"

"Yes! And you need to stand over there and me over here. We shouldn't talk to each other."

She looked at him and started laughing so hard, he saw how hilarious he had just sounded. They got into the van and talked all the way to the hotel. Danny will never forget her saying, "Do you know what my strategy is? If I get on this show, I'm gonna hang on like a hair in a biscuit. You ever seen a hair in a biscuit? It won't come out! There ain't no way to get it out. You just have to throw the biscuit away or eat the hair." Her name was Liz Young.

When they got to the hotel, Danny couldn't leave his room without an escort. He took test after test and filled out all kinds of papers; but he didn't have an interview for three days! He was very worried because he found out that there had already been several interviews. Then, at his first interview, he was asked, "Danny, you said that you used to hide in the closet and eat an entire can of cake frosting, then feel ashamed. Why didn't you just stop?"

Danny tried to answer with some profound analysis, and he came away wondering if he had blown the entire interview. He called Darci in tears, and she said, "You're going to get a second chance. You just have to bring it up a notch and be that joyful, passionate guy we love so much!" On the home front, she and the kids were experiencing one of the longest weeks of their lives. They lived for any communication from Danny, but hearing this was hard.

After Darci's encouraging words, Danny told her he knew what he had to do. He had to bring out every emotion he could. He had to be loud, soft, cry, get mad—bring it all and leave it all on the table in that room! Darci thought, *He's got it all figured out, just like he always does!*

To his relief, Danny was called to another interview. He was with some other contenders in the room, when one guy said, "My goal is to win every challenge on your show!"

At that moment Danny stood up and said, "My goal is to whip that boy's butt!"

"Bring it on!" cried the other guy. As it turned out, this "boy" later made the cast of Season 9! It was Daris George, also from Oklahoma.

Danny felt he had to make one, final impact. He looked at the man who had asked him about eating the cake frosting and said, "You asked me the other day why I just didn't stop. Hell, if I knew that, I wouldn't be sitting here!" Then he began sobbing and said, "I am begging you. Don't send me back to my two-job, bill paying, cesspool of a life; because if you do, I will put me back on a shelf and say, 'I'll take care of you later,' like I have for the past fifteen years! My daughter and my son and my wife are counting on me, and I don't want to die!"

Everyone was silent. The interview ended, and Danny returned to his room. Danny called Darci and said, "I just hit a home run! I knocked it out of the park! I really think this I mine!"

Later that day Danny left for home and was told he would hear from the casting people in a week. Danny did not like leaving without knowing. It scared him. So when he got home, he expended all his nervous energy in filming every minute of his life.

Danny planned a party and was sure to film while everyone waited for the call. Darci said, "There's no way they aren't going to put you on the show!" Danny wasn't so sure.

He and Darci called their families and friends to invite them to the party, and over one hundred people came. They packed the restaurant and waited for the call, which was thirty minutes late! Finally, Danny's phone rang, and the room fell silent. He switched to speakerphone, but it wouldn't work. They heard someone speaking, but he was cutting out! Finally, Danny put the phone to his ear, and everyone waited. Then he yelled, "I'm going!" He raised his hands in the air, Darci, David, and Mary started crying, and everyone in the place went wild.

The next night was Mary Claire's dance recital. Danny was so proud of her. Between numbers, he shared a Coke and a bag of chips with David. He realized how little time he had really spent giving his full attention to either of his children. Suddenly, every moment with them was precious.

During the recital, he got a text from someone he didn't know. Then another, and another, and another. They were all congratulating him and giving him encouraging words before going on the show. He wasn't even supposed to tell anyone he was on the show!

It never occurred that there were over 100 people at the party that heard the call! How could anyone keep that a secret! Later he learned that his friend Arthur had stood up in a full movie theater and said, "Hey everyone! My good friend Danny made it to *The Biggest Loser!*" Then he shouted out Danny's phone number and told them to text him their support. He said, "And tell everyone you know to do it too!"

Since Arthur holds two Guinness World Records, one for the Largest Hand-Squeezed Lemonade and one for the Largest Sweet Iced Tea, this didn't surprise Danny! Crazy seems to be Arthur's middle name! He also needed the encouragement. The next morning, on Mother's Day 2009, Darci and the kids drove him to the airport to catch his flight to Los Angeles.

Because he had so much luggage, they were going to charge him $125, so he decided to leave his guitar at home—a decision he would later regret. Two weeks later, Darci would have to send it to him! (That was when he wrote the song, "Second Chance.") After he went through the security section, he turned and waved until he was out of sight. He had no idea when he would be back.

Despite not knowing when she would see Danny again, Darci drove home feeling more relaxed and confident about their future than ever before. She felt like she could breathe again. And she didn't have time to be sad. The next morning she woke up and heard, "It's time to lose weight."

She jumped out of bed and threw every junk food in the trash. She went to the grocery store and stocked up on healthy food. Although almost fifteen hundred miles apart, she and Danny were each beginning their journey to get healthy—but they were more together than they had been in years. They were one.

Danny would take care of himself.

Darci would take care of herself.

And God would take care of them both.

The Fight Commences

Danny was pre-boarded because of his size. He had two seats again. He asked the flight attendant to film him, which she did. He wanted a record of how big he was on his last plane flight at over 400 pounds! The other passengers who saw this probably wondered what was going on, as no one realized he was going to compete for *The Biggest Loser*. After he landed and got his bags, he was picked up by someone in a van. "Someone in a van" or "Someone I've never met who has an earpiece in their ear" became common friends for the next week, until he learned their names.

The first official weigh-in was held and he was relieved to get it over with. Season 8 would begin the next day. Danny was dismayed when he realized he had already lost 30 pounds, weighing in at 430 pounds. His goal was to lose as much as possible to win. He immediately got on a treadmill. He was so proud to jog 4 of the 20 minutes he was on it. Then he went outside and walked up a very steep hill twice, which was extremely hard. For a while he played one-on-one basketball with a guy named Thai, who beat him mercilessly. Finally, he returned to the hotel and sat in his room. To him, the game was on the moment he weighed in. No more eating junk food. It was time to lose the weight and get healthy!

Being a land surveyor, it was natural for Danny to be exact. He paced from one corner of his room to the other, measuring the distance. Then he began walking back and forth, counting his trips. All the while, he watched the Season 7 Finale. After making a deep line in the carpet, he added up his total trips. He had walked over 1¼ miles. He imagined the people in the room below him were probably thinking, "What in the world is going on up there?" When a 430-pound guy paces back and forth in the room above you, you can hear it!

He laid down to rest, fell asleep, and missed the end of the Season 7 Finale! He didn't know who won until the next morning, when he found out the one he thought would win, Helen, had indeed been the winner. She had been the underdog, but he had seen a drive in her that he knew would bring her to the front. He thought, *My horse won, and now it's my turn!* (He also realized that his gambling terminology was still very much alive!)

Then it was time to go to *The Biggest Loser* ranch, which frightened Danny. The huge mansion they stayed in was awesome, but he was beginning to see the reality of his task. He didn't say much, except to make an occasional humorous observation. He wanted to size up his competition. He also missed his family. When he handed over his cell phone, he realized he would possibly have no contact with them from that moment until he went home.

At least he knew what to expect after watching several seasons of the show, or at least he thought he did. He had seen on television that they weighed in at the end of each week, and everything was measured by the percentage of body weight lost. This made it fair for a person weighing 400 pounds to compete with a person weighing 300 pounds. They got on a scale, which revealed both pounds lost and percentage of body weight lost.

On the big screen where these numbers were posted, there was a yellow line. When all the contestants' weight loss was posted, the two who lost the least percentage of their body weight would usually fall below the yellow line. Then came the elimination. Danny knew by watching previously that those who didn't fall below the yellow line voted on which of the two would be sent home. If it was a tie, the one who had lost the least percentage went home.

He knew that the only way to avoid going home for sure was to win immunity in a challenge. He had seen on seasons 5, 6 and 7 that challenges were random and took place every week. They could be a race or a contest of some kind. The winner got either immunity, a pound advantage on the scale, or some sort of prize. He remembered that there were also temptations. A temptation was a game involving something that would tempt the contestants in some way. Prizes could be money, control of some aspect of the game, or a pound advantage. He remembered punishments for prior seasons could be having to eat a high-calorie food or getting a pound disadvantage.

The seasons Danny had watched were couples seasons, so each contestant came to the ranch with a partner. Since this was a singles season, he thought he wouldn't have a partner, which pleased him. He had always been a "go it alone" type of guy. Then, after the first challenge, they were told they would pick their partners in the order they had finished. Danny finished third to the last, so he knew he wouldn't get to choose. This discouraged him until Liz Young picked him. He wondered if God was trying to tell him that he needed someone by his side to get through this. That thought didn't comfort him! What did comfort him was that he liked Liz and already had gotten to know her a little. In the weeks and months to come, she would prove to be one of the reasons he did so well.

Whenever he thought of Darci and the kids, he became worried and started to cry. Soon he realized he had no idea what they were doing or going through, so he might as well focus completely on what he was supposed to be doing at the ranch. It was still a struggle. Whenever his family came to mind, he had to fight tears and anxiety.

More Than a Workout

The first workout with the trainers proved significant to Danny. During the seminar in Dallas, he had been given the name "Reject." Being analytical, in vain he had tried to figure out why. In the end, he decided it was probably because he had been rejected by some of his family members. He was soon to learn the eye-opening truth.

That first training day, Bob Harper and Jillian Michaels, the trainers on *The Biggest Loser*, worked them hard for hours. The group found out both of them would be their trainers. They put them all on treadmills, and over an hour later, they called Danny for his training session. Over an hour! He had thought he had conquered the world with 20 minutes on the treadmill the day before!

Bob worked Danny and some others on the floor of the gymnasium for what seemed like forever. Then he ended the workout and told everyone to go to the kitchen and eat lunch. Danny turned to go when he heard, "Except you, Danny." Bob worked him for a while longer after everyone else had gone. Now he was beyond exhausted. Four hundred thirty pounds and hours of workouts on the first day? He was hurting all over. It seemed insane to him. He sat on a bench and slid off of it to the ground.

If you watch episode one of Danny's season, you'll see Bob lean over and say to Danny, "I'm never going to let you rest because I have no idea how long you're going to be here. Whether you go home the first week or last the entire season, every day I'm going to make you feel like you're going home tomorrow. Now, get up." And the workout continued.

Bob asked him, "What happened to you?"

"I just gave up. Fifteen years ago, I gave up on music. I gave up on my joy. And I just gave up on me."

"So you've spent the last fifteen years taking care of everyone else and rejecting yourself?"

The light bulb went on. In that moment, Danny finally realized the one who had rejected him all these years was none other than himself! It wasn't anyone in his family. None of his friends. Not even God. He alone was at fault for rejecting who he was and what he desired to do in life. He wished he could tell Darci. She would be so amazed—or maybe she wouldn't!

Bob also said, "Now I'm going to be 'your Danny.' Now I'm going to take care of you."

Danny realized that in serving God all these years, he had merely gone through the motions, and then begrudgingly done what he believed he had to do. He never thought God would or should take care of him. Deep down, he never really believed God loved him or wanted him to be happy. So he had to control everything in his life.

Now, he really saw God as his Father for the first time, and he saw himself through his Heavenly Father's eyes. As a father himself, he knew the heartbreak of watching David suffer when he was sick and seeing both David and Mary in the grips of fear that their family might fall apart. He ached because he was separated from them. For the first time, he really understood how much God loved him, and he reached out to Him in a whole new way.

In the days following the workout, he thought of all the bad decisions he had made because he had blamed his circumstances on someone else, even God. He listed all the things he should have done and all the things he shouldn't have done. For the first time in his life, he was taking responsibility for his actions in a healthy way, and he repented for all his self-destructive and rebellious behavior.

His new relationship with God cleared a path for him to get through that first workout, and then the next, and then the next. At every turn, he saw new possibilities for his life. Every morning he would get up and go to the little wicker basket Beverly, his mother-in-law, had hidden in his suitcase for him before he left home. In the basket were about a hundred cards, each with a verse of Scripture or words of encouragement written on them. He never ceased to be amazed at how the card he read each morning related to what he was thinking, feeling, and going through. And when there was a challenge, it was uncanny how what he had read that morning related to it.

He didn't go to the ranch to preach Jesus to people, but he had a deep desire to "be Jesus" to people. His old problem with being in a contest where someone would win and the rest would lose was still in his heart. He was not out to destroy his competitors. Yes, he wanted to win, but he was determined to do it with love and compassion. Knowing how much God loved him made this easier, especially when tension and tempers rose.

When his roommate and he would wake up in the morning, Danny would him about this daily card challenge prediction phenomenon. Word about this began to get around. When they saw that they were going to have a challenge, his roommate and other contestants would surround him and ask, "What does the scripture say today?"

One contestant was an atheist, and Danny had several discussions with this person about life and relilgion. Then something amazing happened. As Danny showed the daily "word" to the others one day, they all said, "I wonder what that means?"

The atheist saw that everyone actually believed it would predict the challenge and said, "Can I see the scripture?"

Danny decided to have some fun. "Why would you want to see this? You don't even believe in Who said it?"

The atheist sighed and looked at him beseechingly, so Danny showed them the card. Danny thought, *This is awesome, God! An atheist is asking me to share Your Word with them!* When they parted at the end of the season, this person told Danny, "I don't believe in God, but as far as a Christian walk goes, you have the best one I've ever seen."

A Great Comfort

Although Danny isn't sure how long the others on the show worked out, he is sure about his regiment. He averaged 7-9 hours each day. Danny would lie in bed at night totally spent physically, mentally, and emotionally. It would drive him crazy if he thought about Darci and the kids. Were they okay? Were the bills being paid? Was everyone well? Then he would remember what he knew. Just before he had left, his friend Arthur and his wife Noell had promised to help watch over his family. They had also given them some money to help financially. The verse in the Bible that says God helps His children through His other children kept coming back to Danny. It seemed everywhere he turned, God was saying, "Danny, you're not supposed to do life alone."

Then there was their church family. When Darci had had such a breakthrough after the three weekends in Dallas, she went back to church with Danny and the kids on several occasions, but she no longer felt comfortable there. Danny had begun to feel the same way, but he also felt lead to stay at the church until the person who had replaced Orlando as music minister left. He also knew that this person had been told they were going to be replaced after the new year. He knew God wanted him to support them as long as they were there.

In August of 2008, Orlando called from Houston. This wasn't unusual because he and Danny talked regularly. In fact, when Danny would see it was Orlando calling, he would answer, "Hey

OJ! When are you coming back to start your church?" Every time, Orlando would laugh it off, but this time he didn't. God had called him back to the Tulsa area to start a church. Danny and Darci were ecstatic! This was an answer to prayer. The music minister Danny was supporting was about to leave, and they had not felt drawn to any other church. Now they knew why!

Danny resigned from the band, and he and Darci and the kids had fun visiting various churches in the city until Orlando and his family moved back and started holding meetings in their home. Their numbers grew quickly, and by Easter Sunday of 2009, they were in a building and officially launched The Bridge.

His church family had been their spiritual strength through the months he auditioned for *The Biggest Loser*, and Danny knew they were surrounding Darci and the kids with love and everything they needed while he was away. Was he learning to let go and trust God? Had God pulled him completely out of the daily affairs of his home and work to wake him up? He never realized what a tight hold he had had to have on every area of his life. He had to let go of everything to come to *The Biggest Loser!* Now he knew he had to continue to let go so God could help him.

Danny began to see that when he did his part and trusted God, he knew his family would be okay. He could breathe easy. And what he was doing now was all about breathing!

Week Two

After a challenge, the remaining contestants were awarded a call home. This meant more to Danny than any amount of money they might have won, because he hadn't talked to his family for almost 20 days! He wondered how the kids were, if Darci was doing okay, even if the lawn had been mowed! They brought a phone to Danny's room, he dialed the number, and he almost burst out crying when he heard Darci's voice. He blurted out, "How are things? Everything all right? You all right?" She told him they were all fine, the bills were paid, and he didn't have to worry about them. Then he talked to David, "Hey buddy! Are you being the man of the house? I need you to take care of Mary and Mom, okay?"

All Mary had to say was, "Daddy?" and he began to cry profusely. Then they were both crying. She had been one of the biggest parts of his motivation to do this, and every time he felt like he was going to die or he wanted to quit, he saw her beautiful, freckled face.

When Darci got back on the phone she said, "Everything is fine. Just stay there and do what you need to do. Everyone here is praying for you!"

She was telling him the truth. Even with the loss of Danny's salary by taking leave from his job, things were fine; she had picked up some houses to clean and many people were sending money and helping in so many ways. Her friend Tammie often took care of her kids while she was working. Darci was also experiencing what it was like to allow people to help her and to let God take care of her.

She bought Jillian Michaels' book and the pounds began dropping off of her too. Her brother Dan declared he was going to lose weight with Danny, and he challenged the rest of the family to do the same. Now it seemed everyone she knew was eating healthy and working out!

Week Three

Danny was so excited. He no longer had to take any of his medications and was actually seeing a difference in his health. His body was responding to the diet and the workouts, and he was getting well. This was a big motivator. Then his legs swelled with water, and he was worried that they might send him home. He only lost 4 pounds that week because of water retention from edema in his legs. He looked up and said, "I can't go home, God. I haven't done what I need to do yet. It's all up to You."

Because of a turn of events, Danny's weight didn't count that week and Liz's did. In the end, they each stayed on the ranch by a stroke of luck…or a stroke of supernatural intervention!

Week Four

Something bizarre happened. Danny, Liz, and Julio were walking when just to their right, they saw a bird fall from the sky and die on the spot. Not five minutes later, a squirrel fell from a tree and landed flat on its belly in the road. Splat! It scared them to death! They watched as the squirrel hobbled off the road, barely made it over the curb, and crawled away.

Danny said, "Do you think this is a sign? Is one of us going to fall below the yellow line this week?" They had talked about how their main goal was for the three of them to stay above the line together. Then it happened. Out of all possible combinations, all three fell below the yellow line!

The others could either send Liz and Danny home and get rid of two players, or they could send Julio home and only get rid of one player. The obvious, most tactical move would be to eliminate two more people standing in the way of the rest of them winning. Danny was sure he and Liz were going home.

Then another miracle happened. Many people were astonished and said that it was the craziest thing they had ever seen on the show. Danny and Liz would stay another week. Danny knew God was behind that craziness! More and more, he was seeing that when he took his hands off something, did his best, and trusted God, God came through in ways he could never have imagined.

Week Five

Danny was separated from Liz when the entire house was split, and everyone was upset. Danny found himself on a team that didn't know him very well, the Black Team. He hadn't been a part of their circle, and they seemed to have already formed an alliance, which meant they might never vote against each other. He believed they liked him and trusted him, but he would have to work harder than everyone else to stay on the ranch.

That week they had a temptation, and the game involved a gamble. If you played and spun the wheel, you had three possible wins: money, food you had to eat, or ultimate control of the game. Before he had left, Darci and Danny had talked and agreed he shouldn't play any games. He should just work hard, and if they offered him money for a pound, he should take the pound. But his compulsive, controlling nature kicked in, and he was suddenly panicked that someone else might control his destiny if they won control of the game.

Danny stepped up to play. He spun the wheel and won a 780-calorie cupcake, which he now had to eat! Immediately, he began beating himself up for being so stupid. But suddenly he saw something else: He was rejecting himself again. This was exactly why he was here in the first place! All his life he had moved further and further into a dark hole because of regret and unresolved guilt. He was always chasing his losses instead of repenting, forgiving himself, letting it go, and moving on.

He repented for going against his agreement with Darci and gambling. And while he was at it, he forgave himself for the way he had treated her and others through the years. Now he knew God loved him and forgave him—and that made all the difference! He would eat the stupid cupcake and then exercise it off.

Period. He would work harder than ever this week, and then he would trust God for the rest. No other human being could control his destiny unless he let them, and he wanted God to be in control because God knew best.

Later that day, the group went for a hike up the mountain as an extra workout. The younger and less obese usually made it to the top first and would come back down to meet the larger, slower ones. Danny was a larger, slower person. Every hike was a struggle, and he would have to stop periodically to catch his breath. This day was different.

Amanda, a 19-year-old girl from New Jersey, chose to stay with him for the entire hike that day. She took his hand and said, "Danny, today you are going to walk up this hill without stopping. If we have to slow down, we'll slow down together. We just won't stop." She reminded him to control his breathing on that hike, and he remembered how his father (who had COPD) pursed his lips to breathe effectively. For the first time, he made it to the top without stopping! He thanked Amanda for selflessly staying behind and helping him when she didn't have to. He saw what a good heart she had, and in the coming weeks they became very close.

That week they were also were given a chance to win videos from home. Danny's team lost and he was devastated. He wanted to see his family so badly. Although he knew Darci had help, he needed to hear her tell him everything was fine. He was so upset about losing that he walked away from the others with tears streaming down his face. Amanda saw him and walked over to stand beside him. She didn't say a word. She just took his hand.

Danny's former partner, Liz, had won her home video, and she asked Danny to watch it with her. Danny thought, *At least I can share her joy.* They sat on the couch and the video began running. He immediately noticed the little girl in the chair and said, "Liz, your granddaughter looks just like—" and he burst into tears.

It was Mary Claire. Liz had given up her family video so that he could see his family instead! She knew how hard it had been for him to be away from them, and she also felt she needed Danny to stay at the ranch with her. She had worried that he was missing his family so much, he might get sent home. Danny could not thank her enough.

Just as amazing was what was on the video. Darci, David, and Mary recited the words to "My Wish" by Rascal Flatts. It was their prayer for God to help him fulfill his destiny. They couldn't have known that two nights before this, Danny had awakened at two in the morning, had gone into the kitchen, and had written Darci a letter. He was crying so hard that his tears were wetting the paper. Amanda also had awakened and come to get a glass of water. She saw Danny crying and asked if everything was all right. He said, "I'm just missing my family so bad." She smiled and put her hand on his shoulder. And what was he writing to Darci? The words to "My Wish."

His letter and Darci's video had crossed in the mail, but God had been directing both of them. Danny felt honored that in all her years of suffering through his selfishness, temper, and neglect, Darci still wanted what was best for him, no matter what the cost. She had never stopped believing in him. As he listened to the video, he felt the depth of her love and knew he had the greatest wife in the world.

What Danny didn't know was that making this video was Darci's challenge for the week! She had only a few hours to shoot the video and had just finished cleaning a house. It was about 100 degrees in Oklahoma, and she didn't have a video camera. Sweating profusely, she called Tammie, who had loaned her their camera in the past. Tammie rushed right over.

"My Wish" was Darci's song to Danny, so she and David and Mary Claire each recited a portion of the lyrics. Then they told Danny not to worry about them; that they were doing great. They missed him but wanted him to keep doing what he was doing and STAY ON THAT RANCH!

Darci ran to the Federal Express place and sent the tape, never realizing that Danny had no idea it was coming, nor had she received his letter with "My Wish" in it. When she got the letter, she was so deeply touched—again—at how God was working in their lives. And she only knew a part of it. Despite his cupcake escapade, Danny lost in the double-digits that week.

Week Six

The week began with a challenge to dig a hole in the sand and pull out a chest to get a key that was inside. Easier said than done! It took Danny an hour because when he dug so deep, the sand on the sides of his hole would cave in and destroy the progress he had made. He figured out he would succeed if he just didn't quit, and he realized he could apply that to his whole life. He looked back and saw all he might have done if he had not quit in the past. He decided to "lose his quit" forever, and "Lose Your Quit" became his mantra. (www.LoseYourQuit.com)

Danny was the first to dig out his box, but the Black Team lost the challenge. The good news was that the other team chose to send them all home for several days. He would get to see his family! Then he became frightened because he knew he would have to continue to work out just as hard to keep losing the weight and stay on the show. The Blue Team would have no distractions on the ranch, and that concerned him greatly.

When they arrived in Tulsa, the camera equipment did not arrive on the flight. Danny stayed in a hotel and couldn't rejoin his family or even work out until the equipment arrived later that evening. He was extremely agitated, but when he finally saw Darci, David, and Mary Claire, he thought his heart would burst.

When Darci was asked how Danny looked to her, she said, "Great!"

"He's lost a lot of weight, hasn't he?"

She said, "The weight is great, but when I looked into his eyes, I saw that his spirit man was back. I saw the man God created him to be."

Darci was so exhausted, she thought, *Oh my. What did I just say?*

When Darci found out Danny was coming home, she panicked! She switched into high gear and put the word out because she needed help. She had been so busy cleaning other people's houses that her own was a mess. And she was worried they might even inspect their kitchen cabinets and refrigerator!

As usual, her family rallied around and worked feverishly to get the house and yard in good shape. Beverly and Quint came immediately to scrub and clean the house. Her brother Dan did all the yard work and hauled off four truckloads to the dump. Her brother-in-law Bob drove in from Arkansas and spent two days staining the deck. They were like an army of ants that moved a mountain in record time.

The show wanted Danny's arrival to be a surprise to the kids, so Darci was doing all this preparation while trying not to make them suspicious. Danny called before his plane left, and she was so excited. They didn't know the delays they would have to endure, just miles away from each other again, before they would reuinite! When she saw the truck coming down their street, she thought, *Finally!* But she would have to wait another fifty minutes. All this "hurry up and wait" was like torture, but it was worth it when Danny walked through the door seventy pounds lighter (more than he had ever lost before) and with that old sparkle in his eye. There had been times she wondered if she would ever see it again.

They filmed until late in the night, and then Danny finally went to work out. The 24-hour gym was closed, and he almost gave up. "You mean 24-hours except when you need it the most? Why is it like everything is out to keep me from exercising?" When he drove up in the driveway, he got angry. The Blue Team had decided to send him home so he would fail. In that case, he would just have to prove them wrong! The challenge was on - he decided to walk around the neighborhood, which he did for three hours. Darci was awake when he got home because David had been vomiting all night. The poor guy was so sick, he never made it on camera the entire week.

That night, Darci could see the stress in Danny's eyes. He was afraid he would fall behind. He was freaked out that his team was going to vote him off the ranch, and he felt incredible pressure to somehow get immunity. She said, "I'll cook whatever you need to eat, however you need it cooked, and you just concentrate on working out."

His family was very understanding, except for Mary Claire. She missed Danny and had made plans to go to the zoo with Daddy. Mary was always making plans! Danny felt terrible. He knew that his workouts must come first. He told her that every day he worked out now meant more years they would have fun together later. She still hinted that the monkeys would be there if they did decide to go!

Danny was close to GG, Darci's grandmother, and he made sure to call and talk with her before leaving. They always had long talks about everything from politics to finances. Later GG called to tell Darci, "I can tell he's lost weight! He even sounds skinnier!" She used to bribe him with money if he would lose weight. Unfortunately, GG passed away while he was at the ranch. Darci waited to tell him. She knew GG would be so angry if she were the cause of breaking Danny's concentration.

One evening before Danny went back to the ranch, Orlando and their church home group came to pray for him. They prayed for his supernatural weight loss. And then it was time for him to leave. Though the producer may have thought Darci might say something emotional on camera about her dismay with Danny leaving again, she actually said, "I'm not sad. I'm glad he's going back. I didn't even want him to be here in the first place. I want him to be at the ranch losing weight, because that is where he belongs. I'm sorry, but I'm not going to be able to give you tears." The poducer said, "Wow! You may have one of the healthiest perspectives of any spouse I've ever seen on this show!"

Darci knew the only reason she was at all "healthy" was because of all the healing God had done in her heart over the past few years. Nevertheless, she was apprehensive about what would happen when Danny returned to the ranch. Would he immediately be sent home? Worried she might see him again in just a few days, Darci met with Kathy and the prayer group. Darci expressed her concerns, and Kathy said, "I'm believing he will lose 15 pounds and blow everyone's mind!"

Danny got back to the ranch knowing he needed another miracle. He had lost two days in travel and one day at the hotel. He hadn't been able to work out like the others, who had remained on the ranch. Again, he put the whole situation in God's hands and remembered Orlando's prayer, that he would have supernatural weight loss. Of course, he didn't know what Kathy had said until later.

With great trepidation and clinging to his faith, Danny got on the scale. The look on his face was suspense and despair. Then the numbers flashed on the screen and he saw the results. He had lost 15 pounds, more than any other contestant that week – even more than those who had stayed on the ranch! This did blow people's minds! However, Jillian warned him that after two good weight-losses in a row, a low weight-loss week usually followed.

He told her, "No, it's not going to happen."

She said, "Danny, you don't know how this works."

He replied, "Jillian, you don't know how I work!"

She rolled her eyes and said, "Whatever."

Week Seven

This week, Danny's team was planning to send him home. He knew this for certain because he walked in on them having a conversation about it. However, when he got on the scale at the end of the week, he had lost 12 pounds, and again he won immunity.

They had to send one of themselves home. He had had another great week and remembered one of the verses he had pulled out of Beverly's box: "When evil men advance against me to devour my flesh, when my enemies and my foes attack me, they will stumble and fall" (Psalm 27:2 NIV).

Meanwhile, Darci was back in her routine also. Her sister Dacri and her nephew came to visit during the Fourth of July holiday. Late that night, after the kids were in bed, she and Dacri got in the pool for a while and talked. Darci began to cry. "You know, I've always just wanted him to lose the weight and be healthy and happy, but now I really want him to win. I want him to feel like a champion for once."

Dacri said, "Look at that star! It's a sign that he's going to win. And every time you doubt it, you're going to look up at the sky and see a star and know he's going to win! You're going to look up and trust God. He is in control."

Week Eight

This week the contestants went to Washington, D.C. They had lunch at the White House, met senators and congressmen, and made the case that obesity has become a national epidemic. Although Darci knew Danny was travelling with the show to Washington D.C., she knew she still wouldn't be able to talk with him.

Not long after that, she got a call from a friend who had been surfing the Internet. She said, "Darci, I am looking at a picture of Danny by the Washington Monument! Go there and look at it!" Darci grabbed her laptop and went to the site. The contestants had done a public workout, and some of those who had watched had posted pictures of it. For the first time, she saw a huge difference in Danny's weight, which really excited her.

One day the contestants met in front of the Jefferson Memorial. The first thing Danny noticed was a table with a cloth over it. He elbowed Liz, "Do you know what's under there?"

She asked, "What?"

He said, "Our brown shirts."

God had delivered him from the Black Team and they were all single contestants again. His fate would no longer be decided by a political process, alliances and team voting. He would continue to work as hard as he could, but he was relieved to know the rest was solely between him and God.

On the last day, in front of the Lincoln Memorial, they had the week's weigh-in. Danny had lost another 12 pounds, after again being told he might have a low weight-loss! He also lost more than anyone else—again. Between this victory and being released from the Black Team, he looked up at Lincoln and thought, *So this is what it's like to be emancipated.*

Week Nine

Back at the ranch, Danny and Shay both lost 17 pounds in week nine – more than anyone else. But because Shay lost less in percentage of body weight, she was sent home. Danny hated that someone who lost as much as he did still left the ranch. Life at the ranch was still hard work, but he had moved into a routine. He felt like a motor that was running on all cylinders. More than anything, he felt the favor and strength of God working in him to do what he was doing. He never felt closer to his Heavenly Father.

Week Ten

This was the makeover week. Unbeknownst to Danny, Darci and the kids were on their way to Los Angeles to surprise him. In 48 hours, Darci had to clean two houses, get everyone's hair cut, and buy new clothes for the trip. She had gone from a size 24 to a size 14, and nothing in her closet fit! She was exhausted but excited by the time they boarded their plane early in the morning.

"Someone they didn't know with an earpiece" picked them up at the airport and took them to the hotel, where they had a swim and met the families of the other contestants. The next morning they got to go to CityWalk at Universal Studios, and then it was time to surprise Danny. As it turned out, they stayed in the green room for hours before it was their turn. They were last, and they were learning about how filming television worked!

Meanwhile, hair stylists came to do the contestants' hair and a fashion expert dressed them after they had lost so much weight. After getting his hair colored and his grey removed, Danny walked out on stage to speak to Tim Gunn, the fashion expert. Tim asked him to turn around, and there were Darci, David, and Mary Claire! After hugs and kisses all around, they watched while Danny gave a short speech to an audience about the importance of who you are to the people around you – a foreshadowing of the speaking career Danny would have after the show ended.

Darci and the kids spent two days with Danny at the ranch, so they got to see a little of what Danny had been going through and experience some of it for themselves. They hiked, worked out together, and even stood on *The Biggest Loser* scale together. Unlike the other contestants, however, Danny wasn't sparing any extra time for his family. He stuck to his workout schedule.

Darci felt jealous of his time and realized how much she was missing him. She also realized that for the first time since they had met, he was experiencing something she wasn't. He was becoming really close to all these people she barely knew. She felt left out and left behind. She had to fight her emotions and remind herself that he was doing all this for them.

She also had no idea how used to the obese Danny she had become. She was shocked that the thinner Danny seemed so foreign to her. In fact, it scared her. One day it would be over and he would come home. But would he be so changed that he wouldn't want her anymore? Old lies of not being pretty enough haunted her again.

One night as they were about to go to sleep, Darci decided it was time to tell Danny that GG had died. At first he was upset that they hadn't called him, but then he understood their reasons. She told him that everyone in the family was in the room for GG's last moments, and she began weeping. Danny asked, "What's wrong?"

Darci replied, "Nothing. I'm just thinking about GG." But she was really wondering if she was losing Danny.

Whenever they worked out together, she doubled her efforts to do well, and several times Danny complimented her. This made her feel good, but she cried tears of worry when she and the kids left for the airport. As it turned out, they missed their flight, which gave them a five-hour layover. She decided to take the kids to the beach. David and Mary got to play in the ocean for the first time. As she sat in the warm sun and watched them, she felt God's goodness in this little, extra blessing. She knew He was trying to tell her that their lives were safe in His hands.

What Darci didn't see was that her visit was just what Danny needed to motivate him to finish strong. Now there were six contestants left, and only four would go to the finals, so Danny worked even harder. He and Liz would wake up and sneak out before everyone else even woke up to walk. God told him to get a workout in before anyone else did. That way, the others would unknowingly be playing catch up all day.

At the end of the week, Rebecca, who was one of the biggest threats, was voted off. She did amazing and won the $100,000 home prize. They also did a photo shoot that week for a major magazine. It was the first time Danny had ever been in a major magazine spread.

Week Eleven

They were down to five contestants, and Danny was now fighting to be in the final four. With her roommate Rebecca gone, Amanda talked with Danny even more. He had such respect for her. She had defied the odds by getting to the ranch at all. Losing weight was harder for her because she had a medical condition in her legs called Lipedema. Lipedemic fat cannot be lost through diet or exercise, so she was at a disadvantage.

More and more, Danny felt like a father figure to Amanda. That feeling was sealed one night when he was in the laundry room and heard her scream, "Danny! Where are you! I need you! My daddy's not here!"

He looked into the hall to see a soaking wet Amanda in a towel. "What in the world is going on here?"

Amanda explained, "My shower overflowed into the entire room, and I don't know what to do!" They both laughed hysterically.

Danny worked hard with Amanda and Liz, taking Amanda under his wing. He encouraged her, and he secretly prayed for her to stay above the yellow line so she could remain at the ranch.

By now he was working out up to 12 hours daily, more than he ever had before. He wasn't about to get this far and not make the final four! He lost 16 pounds and did make it to the final four. Both Amanda and Liz did as well. Danny went home tied for the lead with Rudy, and he was happy for his friends. Now they would all face the challenge of continuing to lose weight at home for about four months.

Running for Gold

Danny was sure his homecoming would be filmed, and footage would be aired on national television; but that was not his main concern. While she was at the ranch, Darci had said, "You're going to get good looking and leave me." She had said this like a joke, but Danny saw through it. He knew she was worried about their relationship. Both of them had gone through tremendous changes in the past few months.

His first priority was to put Darci's heart at ease. When he walked in the door and their family and friends were there, the first thing he did on national television was walk up to Darci and kiss her. He turned to the crowd and announced, "As hard as this has been on me, it has been even harder on someone else." He took

Darci's hand, gave her a bracelet, and asked her to remarry him and renew their vows. She had stood with him through fifteen years of hell, and he was so grateful. He loved her so much. She was the most beautiful woman he had ever known, inside and out, and he wanted her to know how lucky he felt that she had stayed with him.

Darci was overwhelmed. She threw her arms around Danny and kissed him, so grateful to God for such a wonderful guy. They had come a long way! She was still concerned about his time at home, however. She and the kids had their routine and he had his routine. Would their lives fit together again?

And poor David! He barely made it to his father's homecoming at all. Darci's dad had had to rush him to the minor emergency clinic to get a shot. He was breaking out in a rash all over his body, which turned out to be poison ivy. David dubbed this the "curse of the camera crew"! He was rarely filmed—again. The last time it was because of throwing up all night, and now because of a rash. This was regretful as David is so interesting, but Mary Claire made up for her brother's absence with her outgoing personality.

Before Danny returned, Darci had lost a lot more weight. The treadmill had become her new best friend. One day she heard God say, "You're a runner."

She said, "I hate running."

Then she heard it again: "You're a runner."

She would find out what this meant soon.

The camera crew left and Danny began the hard task of working out at home. Three days after that, he quit his job. He knew his job now was to win the show, and he needed both the time and the ability to concentrate on nothing but that. His bosses were more than understanding. They told him that when he was finished, his job would be there if he still wanted it.

He prayed for God to provide what his family needed to survive, and God had already tapped Arthur and Noell on their shoulders again. They had contacted friends and family and requested that they send any money they could to help Danny and Darci get through the next few months. They even received a check for $5 from a retired woman in Minnesota! Arthur also told them to send cards of encouragement, even if that was all they could give.

People didn't just give money. When Danny and Darci needed a gas grill to cook chicken breasts, the word went out and a grill appeared in their driveway. Arthur owned a Chick-fil-A restaurant, so they never had to worry about chicken. Personal trainers Miranda and Levi trained Danny without charge. Arthur gave him a mountain bike to ride back and forth to the gym. Others gave him free memberships to their gyms. Tom, a local chiropractor, gave Danny treatments, and Marsha, a massage therapist, gave Danny a free massage every single week!

Orlando put the word out in the church, and money and cards started coming in from everywhere. The money was incredible, but the cards of encouragement were priceless. Danny and Darci had the same feeling they had had when everyone at the seminar held them up. They felt loved, and they knew they weren't alone in this fight.

Danny was so excited to see that Darci had lost 47 pounds by the time he came home. For the first time, he felt like he was providing the right leadership for his wife and family. He learned that when he had left for Los Angeles, Darci's brother Dan had challenged the whole family to lose weight along with Danny. It seemed like everyone he knew had slimmed down! He thought, *Wow! God gave me Genesis 50:20 for all this, and we are already seeing other people's lives changing for the better!*

Then they found out that Danny would be running a marathon, which intimidated him. He thought about finding a running partner for the race who could support him. Darci suggested his trainer Miranda or his cousin Sarah, who had run several marathons. Danny looked at her and said, "Wait a minute – that would be ridiculous. You need to do this with me." They began training for it together, and Darci knew—like it or not, she was a runner!

Darci's problem was that she hadn't worked out since Danny had returned. Without even praying, the answer presented itself. Marsha had been giving Danny a weekly massage, but she was also a personal trainer. Marsha told Danny that God had told her to help him, and Danny asked her if she could train Darci and help her continue with her weight loss. Marsha agreed, and she and Darci became great friends and prayer partners. Now Darci went into strict training.

Darci had already agreed to minister at a women's retreat, so during it she continued to train and even brought her own food. There was a special time during the retreat when each woman picked a random scripture written on the leaves of a fake tree. Darci's scripture was 1 Corinthians 9:24-25 in The Message, which says, "You've all been to the stadium and seen the athletes race. Everyone runs; one wins. Run to win. All good athletes train hard. They do it for a gold medal that tarnishes and fades. You're after one that's gold eternally." That day she ran 6.5 miles without stopping for the first time. She knew that passage of Scripture was speaking to her about their entire life together, not just about the marathon or *The Biggest Loser*.

After several months, it was time to fly out to run the marathon. Danny was also to weigh-in and see if he made it to the final two. Danny wondered if he should work out extra hard and sweat the night before. He called Bob Harper to ask his opinion, who said, "When you see the others, you'll know what you should do."

When Amanda, Liz, and Rudy came to Danny and Darci's room, they gasped. Rudy said, "Man, you won this!" Danny looked at them and thought it might be true. He had lost 59 pounds in the 60 days he had been off the ranch. After they left, Darci asked, "Are you going to work out?"

Danny said, "I'm going to bed." That night he made a wise decision. He would run the marathon with extreme caution, even walking if necessary, to keep from jeopardizing his health and progress on the show.

The marathon went well. The last few miles were run along the beautiful Pacific Coast Highway. Darci had been with Danny since mile 13. When they hit the stretch along the ocean, she felt so free! The waves and the sea lions were awesome to watch. She thought, *We are free of the weight and the burdens of the past. Nothing will ever be the same.*

After the marathon they returned to Tulsa and, again, Danny remained completely focused; but this time Darci felt a part of the process. There were some sweet moments with the kids too. One day, Danny was running on the treadmill and David was sitting on the couch next to him. They were watching the current episode of *The Biggest Loser*, which was filmed when Danny weighed 400 pounds. David looked at Danny on the television and then looked at him running now, at about 225 pounds. He turned back and forth a couple of times, and Danny took notice. A tear was running down David's cheek.

He asked, "What's wrong?"

"Dad, no one loses weight like that!"

Danny replied, "Your father does."

Danny's thoughts went back in time to the school carnival. David couldn't find him and had asked Darci, "Where's Dad?"

Darci answered, "He's working one of the rides."

David murmured, "Great."

"Why did you say that?" asked Darci.

David blurted out, "They're all going to make fun of him!"

Danny remembered how hurt he had been when Darci had told him. He thought, *Thank God those days are over!*

Jillian's Gift

Jillian Michaels came to Oklahoma to visit Danny and work him out. Danny often joked to Darci about how he thought Bob Harper was so tough, but on this particular day Jillian was relentless! She wore him down in the gym, and when he had to stop, they talked. She asked him about his father. Danny just began to weep. "I always thought the weight was the issue, but I realize now it never was; it was the symptom of the issue." He told her he grew up always craving attention and never got enough. He always tried to be the best, like his father, who was his hero.

She said, "Your father didn't love you very much, did he?"

For a moment Danny was offended. Then he knew she meant that his dad hadn't physically or verbally expressed his love for him very often. Yes, that had been a deep wound. As a result, he had spent his whole life trying to be a hero like his dad, to win his love and approval. He had pursued this so diligently that he had forfeited the life God had given him to live. He had rejected the person God created him to be. Of course he became sick!

There was more. He realized that in a twisted way, he believed he couldn't pursue his dreams and be successful because, in his eyes, his father had never done that. If Danny had run after the desires of his heart and succeeded, it would have been like putting his father down. He used to think *Why isn't what my father has good enough for me?* The irony was that because he chose to "be his father" and become a land surveyor like him, he spiraled into a course of self-destruction through eating and gambling, which had devastated his father.

This was a huge revelation to Danny. For years, he had been under a web of lies that perversely bent the truth and caused him to make wrong decisions. He looked back over his life and saw how God had tried to help him, even when he was on the wrong path. And now he knew he could live differently. He could stay healthy. He could write music. He could live his dreams.

Danny cried and thanked Jillian for being so honest. During the workout she gave him that day, he lost a lot more than just physical weight!

Season 8 Finale

Just before Danny left for the finale, Arthur and Noell had a party. Many of the attendees had gone through the seminar in Dallas because of Danny and Darci, and now they had a surprise for them. They played "My Wish" and told Danny and Darci to hug each other. Then they lifted them together, just as they had been lifted separately before. They looked at each other. No words could express what they were feeling.

Danny went back to Los Angeles for the final weigh-in. Each of the final four—Danny, Rudy, Liz, and Amanda—stayed in different hotels. None of them knew how much the others had lost since the marathon.

Darci, David, and Mary, were staying with Danny. The night before the final weigh-in, Beverly and Quint had David and Mary spend the night at their hotel so Danny could work out all night. They even snuck a bicycle into the hotel room and assembled it there. Danny began working out, but after fifteen minutes, Danny turned to Darci and said, "I'm tired. I'm going to go to bed."

Darci was surprised. "What if Rudy beats you by one pound?" (At that point, they suspected Amanda and Liz were trailing behind Danny and Rudy.)

Danny sighed, "Sweating isn't real weight loss, and I've done everything I can. If I don't win, then fine. I'm sure he's sweating out, but I'm not going to. I've done the work every day. There's no need to do more now." He was thrilled that Rudy and Liz and Amanda were there at the end. He knew they had all done their best. For the first time in his life, he had no regrets. That was a major victory! And win or lose, he would be okay.

The next evening was the Season 8 Finale. Everyone was filled with anticipation and excitement as the results were revealed: Danny had lost 239 pounds, 5 more pounds than Rudy, and 14 pounds more than he needed to win the show; he had lost 55.58 percent of his body weight, which was 1.1 percent more than any other contestant in the history of the *The Biggest Loser!*

Danny and his family cried and shouted when he won, and there were loved ones, friends, and fans all over Oklahoma and around the world doing the same thing. It was an amazing achievement, especially since Season 8 was also the shortest in the history of the show.

At this writing, Danny holds the record for being The Biggest Loser EVER!

A New Beginning
Every Day

The moment Danny won *The Biggest Loser*, Darci, David, and Mary Claire stormed the stage and almost tackled him. They barely had time to congratulate him with kisses and hugs before he was whisked away. Immediately, he was in a media blitz. This wasn't surprising, because it seemed that every person who had watched that season loved Danny. He spent two hours on the stage, giving interviews.

One of the most memorable interviews was with Ross, from *The Tonight Show with Jay Leno*. He asked Danny, "What are you going to do with the money?"

Without hesitation, Danny said, "I'm going to buy new carpet." When Ross looked shocked Danny continued, "For years we have had the worst carpet, and we need new floors." When they moved into their house, all the windows were broken and animals had lived in the house. They had had the carpet cleaned twice professionally and disinfected, but it was terribly stained.

He and Darci had always said, "When we get out of debt, the first thing we're going to do is buy new carpet!"

When this interview with Ross aired, Danny and Darci were bombarded by different companies who wanted to give them free carpet or wood flooring. They decided on the first company who called. They picked out carpet for the bedrooms and office, and chose wood flooring for the kitchen, living, and dining rooms at a local store. Now their floors are beautiful!

Ross also asked Danny, "Is this the first time you had to lose to win?"

Danny replied, "I think so." His answer never set right with him. A few days later, after he returned to Tulsa, he knew why. He had to lose to win when he accepted Jesus years before.

As soon as all the interviews on the stage were completed, Danny went directly to the airport to catch a red-eye flight to New York City. He left at 10 p.m. and arrived at 6 a.m. He tried to sleep on the plane, but his adrenaline was running high. He also was disappointed that Darci wasn't with him. By the time he landed in New York, he was exhausted.

In the next few days Danny appeared on the *Today* show, *Live with Regis and Kelly*, and many other talk shows, as well as shooting several magazine layouts. He was even the "Milk Mustache" guy in the *USA Today* full page ad! While he was busy with the whirlwind tour, Darci and the kids were having a vacation in California. They went to Lego Land and Sea World. It was very cold, but they had a fantastic time. By the time they got home, Danny was there. They were so glad to see each other and catch up on each other's activities. He told them that one day he had done thirty radio interviews in a row! He found all this exhausting, but he was having a great time.

The Best Christmas Ever

Every year since they had been married, Christmas was hard. They struggled to find the funds to buy gifts for each other, their family, and their friends. Year after year they would receive such nice things from others and could only give so little in return. Then there was Danny's weight. He could never get on a ladder to hang lights on the outside of the house. He would hold the ladder while Darci and David climbed up to do the work.

This year was completely different!

Danny couldn't wait to hang the lights himself. Before he could, a lighting company offered to decorate their house. They put up incredibly beautiful new lights, in blue and white, which were their favorite Christmas light colors. Danny and Darci and the kids were able to go Christmas shopping and bless their family and friends like they had always wanted to through the years. And people from all over the nation were sending them wonderful gifts.

On Christmas Eve, a snowstorm covered the ground with white. They spent the most peaceful, wonderful Christmas Day, exchanging gifts they never could have imagined a year before.

The greatest gift seemed to come right down from Heaven like the powdery snow. After several years of frenzy to get on *The Biggest Loser* and win it, and after so many years of turmoil and change in their family, they basked in the quiet company of each other.

They needed the respite, because when they resumed their new life together, Danny was recognized everywhere they went. On one occasion, he and Darci were on an airport shuttle bus. It stopped to pick up a lady, who sat next to Danny. She began talking about this problem and that problem, facing straight ahead. Then she looked at his face and shrieked! It scared Darci, but it didn't faze Danny. The woman grabbed him, hugged him, and began sobbing. She told him she had lost 60 pounds because of him.

Danny later told Darci that this had become commonplace to him. However, neither of them have ever become used to how Danny's time on *The Biggest Loser* and their story as a couple continues to change people's lives. Although they are often followed in airports, spoken to in restaurants, and followed around when taking their kids different places, they enjoy and are humbled by all these opportunities to help other people realize their dreams.

New Year, New Life, New Challenges

Danny Cahill hit the ground running in 2010. Organizations, businesses, and churches across the nation wanted him to speak, so he began taking lessons in public speaking. His speaking coach at the time introduced him to Jim Stovall, who gave him valuable counsel in public speaking and his new career. Jim wrote the best selling novel and award winning movie, *The Ultimate Gift*, as well as other incredible projects. At the time, Jim was involved in making the movie, *A Christmas Snow*, which was being filmed in Tulsa. He asked Danny to play the part of the food critic, and Danny was delighted. He joined the Screen Actors Guild, got to be a part of a feature film, and never had so much fun! Since then the director, Tracy Trost, also asked Danny to take part in *The Lamp*, and Danny even looks forward to further television and movie projects in the future!

The Doctors television show also called in January. They wanted Danny to do a piece on his skin issue. One of the questions people asked most frequently was, "What happened to all of your skin?" After losing 239 pounds, he had a massive amount of loose skin hanging on his body. Danny agreed to do the show, and during the interview they offered to perform surgery to remove the excess skin, so their viewers could see the difference in his body. Danny was so excited, but he and Darci would have a few adventures before he had the surgery in June.

At the end of January, he had the honor and privilege to play against the Harlem Globetrotters on the Washington Nationals team, which turned out to be one of the most exhilarating times of his life. They played the game in Tulsa, and he was glad for the hometown advantage! He was wondering if he could still shoot after all these years—especially after the senseless beating he had endured from Thai just before *The Biggest Loser*.

They put Danny in the game in the second quarter. He dribbled down the court and tried to figure out what to do next. Just then Big Easy, a famous player for the Globetrotters and fellow reality star from the *The Amazing Race,* yelled, "Take the shot!" Danny immediately made the throw from outside the three-point line. He silently prayed for it just to hit the rim, but *SWISH!* It went in! The crowd went wild. Later in the game, Big Easy literally tackled Danny to the ground, which gave him a free throw. He made a foul shot, and so his final point score was four, which was more than he scored against Thai in their game of 21 a year before! The evening was even sweeter because his family had driven up from Oklahoma City to see the game.

In February, he and Darci flew to Washington, D.C., where Danny spoke at Chick-fil-A's national seminar. They were so impressed with the seminar and how the company operated and took great care of their operators. Then, in March, Danny was invited to speak at Bob Harrison's annual meeting in Maui. Darci went with him, and it was like a second honeymoon. They spent five days at the Regency Hyatt Hotel, and Darci got to hear Danny speak twice. She marveled at how relaxed he was and what interesting things he had to say. The audience responded warmly to him, and she knew he was doing exactly what he was supposed to be doing. She was so proud of him!

One evening they had a nice dinner in a beautiful restaurant. They had no idea "someone" was watching. As they were flying back to Tulsa, they saw a Google alert. Evidently, a newspaper had published everything they ate. That was not what upset Danny, however. The paper had reported that he had been seen with "his girlfriend"! He called the restaurant to ask for a public apology and then called the paper to print it. He wanted them to set the record straight: That amazing-looking woman with him was his wife!

He and Darci later laughed about their first negative encounter with media gossip, and they weren't surprised someone had thought Danny was out with a mistress. How many couples who have been married as long as they have and have been through what they have been through look like starry-eyed lovers? To them, the newspaper article only illustrated how far they had come.

April was a special time for Darci. Since Danny had asked her to remarry him and renew their vows, David's Bridal flew her and Danny to New York City to choose a wedding dress. They walked into their hotel room to see a spread of goodies, just for Darci, all over the bed. It included a jeweled crown, a bright orange bag with an umbrella, makeup, chocolates, and flowers—everything to make her feel like a queen.

That week was a magical week. They jogged along West Side Highway in the afternoon, stopping along the way to set the automated timer on their camera to take pictures of themselves. They ended up over four miles from their hotel, but that was no longer a big deal! They jogged back with no problem.

When Darci had chosen a dress and was being fitted at David's Bridal, the camera crew for Access Hollywood showed up. They filmed her all day and finally Danny came in to see her. It was like a fairy tale! She felt and looked so beautiful. Later, they went to the park, where a photographer for *In Touch Weekly* did a photo shoot. The paparazzi hid in the bushes, taking pictures of Darci. They were all saying, "Who is this woman? Is she an actress?" Danny watched and smiled as everyone treated his wife like a star and ignored him. They were seeing what he had always seen. He was so proud that his being on *The Biggest Loser* was providing her the great experiences he had always felt she deserved.

That evening they had dinner at Gotham Restaurant. They enjoyed the meal and the wonderful atmosphere, even though they had arrived completely soaked after standing in the rain, trying to get a cab. The waiter told them they were seated in the prime spot, Matthew Broderick and Sarah Jessica Parker's table!

The next morning they took a train to Boston, where they joined some of the other *Biggest Loser* contestants and winners. Danny and the others were going to run the Boston Marathon. Darci jumped in at mile 19 and Amanda was there at mile 22. They were laughing and waving their arms while Danny was in terrible pain! Still, he ran it in five hours, eight minutes, coming in second among his *Biggest Loser* compatriots.

As Danny was speaking at various events, he wrote more songs and began to sing them when he spoke. He also recorded a CD, which included, "Reach for It," "Too Many Reasons," and the song, "Second Chance," which he wrote while on the set of *The Biggest Loser*. It even aired on the show when he performed it to the other contestants! He was finally beginning to realize his dreams in writing, performing, and producing music again.

At the end of April, Danny and Darci flew to Nashville, where Danny was going to be a guest on the *Praise the Lord* program at the Trinity Broadcasting Network (TBN). His new friend, Rice Broocks, would be the host of the show. When they arrived at Rice's home, Danny was feeling sick, and he threw up for the first time in twenty-two years! Although it turned out to be nothing, this alarmed Darci, who had never seen him sick like this.

Danny somehow pulled himself together, because that night Rice threw a party for them. Christian music producers, pastors, and many other wonderful people attended. Rice played a video that showed Danny's (and his family's) journey through *The Biggest Loser*. A woman spoke up right afterward and said, "You've got to write a book!" Danny said that he was working on it, and she pointed to Darci and him, "You've got to write a book with your wife!" The woman was Stormie Omartian, author of *The Power of a Praying Wife* and many other books.

Stormie was the first person who saw Darci's much bigger role in Danny's new work. Danny, of course, had been trying to tell Darci this for some time! He knew she was going to write their story with him. He also knew she should begin speaking with him. As others encouraged her, she agreed to speak here and there, and she found that she liked it. It took a couple of years, but she eventually recognized that God was placing her in this new role. Now, she loves to travel with Danny, and they will speak and sometimes sing and play his music together. Another dream come true!

In June 2010, Danny and Darci flew to Palm Springs where he was to have the skin removal surgery. Darci's mother stayed with the children, and they were always so grateful for her help. They never had to worry when she was there! They got to stay at the wonderful Miramonte Resort, which they enjoyed despite Danny's painful recovery.

Danny was excited as the doctors did all the preparatory work. They drew all over his body, fashioning a new suit of skin. When it was time to do the operation, he only had a minute of fear, which was when they strapped him down on the operating table. He felt claustrophobic, and then the anesthetic kicked in and he was asleep.

Although Danny felt like he woke up a few seconds later, he had been on the operating table for eight hours! He was in immense pain and had eight drainage tubes coming out of his body. He continued to experience pain for the next four to five days and was glad Darci was with him. They were able to go back to the resort, where Danny continued to recover. Two weeks after the surgery, he was ready to go home. Doctors Andrew Ordon and Ritu Chopra of The Plastic Surgery Institute, and all of the staff there, were amazing. They stitched up Danny so well that the scars are almost imperceptible. He healed so quickly, two months later he dropped his car off at the mechanic's and jogged four miles home!

In July, Danny had a speaking engagement in Wisconsin and took the entire family for a vacation. They stayed in an RV, which they parked near a small, natural lake. They had a fantastic time. Danny and David got up early one morning to go fishing. They watched as deer played on the other side of the lake. When the sun began coming up, a bald eagle circled, dove into the water, and then rose back up with a fish in its mouth. They caught so many fish that they had a fish fry for dinner that night.

In August 2010, Danny returned to *The Doctors* for the "after surgery" piece. Again, he would take his shirt off on national television. When he did, he was actually in the best shape since the end of the *The Biggest Loser*, and his torso certainly looked better!

The year ended with a great treat. Danny and Darci had loved spending their honeymoon in Florida and had always wanted to take David and Mary Claire to Disney World. They had promised them that if Danny won *The Biggest Loser*, they would go. Christmas of 2010, it was going to happen. They had their friend Mike dress up as Santa and make a special DVD. Several days before Christmas, David found it in the mail. It was addressed to him and Mary Claire, saying: "Play Immediately."

David brought the DVD inside and said, "What is this?"

Danny said, "I don't know. Looks like you better put it in and watch it."

Mary Claire and David sat in front of the television and pressed play. Danny and Darci had secretly placed video cameras in position to record their reactions, which did not disappoint them.

The kids watched as Mike appeared as Santa and cried, "Ho! Ho! Ho! Merry Christmas David and Mary Claire! I've been looking in my book, and your names are in here, but I can't come to your house this year."

Their stricken faces said, *Why? Why can't you come?*

"I can't come to kids' houses when they stay up past midnight!"

Mary Claire looked fiercely at David and elbowed him.

Santa continued, "But that's not why. I can't come to your house because you're not going to be home. You're going to be at Disney World!"

Disappointment turned to tears of joy, and the whole family packed and drove to Orlando for five fabulous days at Disney World. The weather was perfect. It didn't rain until they drove away from the park for the last time. As far as Danny and Darci were concerned, the funniest thing that happened was at the end of a full day of rides and fun. It was dark, and they were standing in a long line to go on a ride. David and Mary Claire sat on the ground and began whining, "Mom! Dad! Let's leave. We're tired. We can't go any more!" Danny and Darci looked at each other, smiled, and shook their heads. Two years before, they couldn't keep up with them...now the tables were turned!

Renewal and Restoration

By 2011, the Cahill family knew they were in an entirely new rhythm of life. Danny spent more time with them, but he was traveling nearly every weekend to speak, and sometimes Darci went with him. When he could, he took one of the kids. He flew over one hundred times in 2010 and again in 2011, but he and Darci were having the time of their lives, doing what they loved to do.

All the changes in their family over the previous years had been tough on David and Mary Claire, but Danny and Darci have so much more to give them now. They are normal kids, who have good days and bad days. Sometimes they say or do things that make their parents cringe—oh, the joys of parenting!—but most of the time they make their parents so proud. They have such a simple trust in God, and that inspires Danny and Darci every day.

When they are at home, Danny and Darci have the joy of playing and singing together, doing praise and worship at their church. They began their relationship performing together, and now they are playing and singing to the Lord together.

In June 2011, Danny and Darci renewed their vows on Victoria Beach, in Laguna Beach, California. It reminded them of when they ran their first marathon, which ended nearby on the Pacific Coast Highway. They rented a house for eight days and brought with them Darci's mother and their pastors, Orlando and Kim, as well as their children. Orlando conducted the ceremony, which was beautiful. The photographer was so moved that he cried. He was another person who was changed by their story.

The ocean crashed onto the rocks while they made their vows to each other. They renewed their life-long commitment, which really had begun when they had met. That seemed like another lifetime. They looked back and saw that they had come out of darkness into the light. How miraculously God had transformed them as individuals and as a couple! With real joy, they looked forward to everything He would do in the future.

They had always wanted to go on foreign missions trips, and that dream began to come to pass with a trip to Thailand, where they served as music ministers for a retreat. They found themselves on the other side of the world singing and ministering to missionaries who needed to be refreshed. Many of them had lived on the mission field for twenty or thirty years, and one couple had been there for over fifty years. They were so grateful, but Danny and Darci were too. They heard so many wonderful stories of God's goodness and faithfulness in these people's lives. Since then, they have performed and ministered at these "In Dew Time" retreats with their friends Steve and Rita Andrew, in several other countries. The difference the retreats make to these sometimes tired laborers is yet another way to make a difference in a world of need.

Steve and Rita listened to their story one night. They said, "Joyce Meyer has got to hear this! Her ministry provides books in the languages of the countries we visit." It wasn't long before Danny and Darci appeared on Joyce's television program, and they told of the significant part she played in how they "went through that mountain" of debt.

Danny and Darci not only saw their own lives renewed and restored. Other people were renewing their dreams and seeing them come to pass. Some of this occurred as their old friends began to meet their new friends. One of the most notable examples was their friend Marsha, who had given Danny free weekly massages during *The Biggest Loser* and also had trained Darci.

The third time Darci trained with Marsha, she looked deep into Marsha's eyes and said, "You're unable to have babies, aren't you?"

Tears came to Marsha's eyes. "How do you know that?"

"God has been speaking to me about it. He's going to give you a baby."

Marsha poured out her heart to Darci. She told her that she and her husband had gone through fertility treatments and were still unable to conceive. They knew it was God's desire for them to have a baby and considered adoption. They had reached the conclusion that conceiving a child might not be in God's plan for their lives, but it was her heart's desire. Darci asked her to join her prayer group, which Marsha did, and they all began praying for her to have a baby.

Soon after, God sent Marsha a friend who was a female obstetrician. She offered to treat her without charge! Tests showed

Marsha had endometriosis. The doctor performed surgery but told her the chances were slim she would get pregnant. Three months later, Marsha and her husband were pregnant! They soon had a healthy, happy baby boy.

Then there was Amanda from *The Biggest Loser*. She still comes to visit Danny and Darci from time to time and is like family to them. When a church in Ohio wanted Danny to speak, they requested he bring another contestant from *The Biggest Loser*. There were a couple of reasons Danny suggested Amanda. He had noticed that she had been quoting Scripture on Facebook and Twitter. She had also picked up Danny's Bible to read from time to time. Once, she remarked that she loved the way it had two translations side by side. When Noell wanted to buy Amanda a gift for her birthday, Danny suggested she get her a Bible like his, and Amanda was thrilled to receive it.

The church in Ohio booked Amanda, who met Danny and Darci there. She spoke before Danny, and for about ten minutes she seemed to be having a little trouble. Then she stopped, took a deep breath, and said, "This is the first time I have ever spoken in a church. I want you all to know that I have just recently found Christ, and the reason is sitting right there: Danny and Darci. When I get around them, I just want to be like them. They make me feel great and positive, and I just wanted what they had. As a result, I'm here in Ohio, speaking in this church and telling you this."

A few moments later she said thank you and walked off the stage. Danny and Darci were in tears. Danny was especially touched. He had always felt jealous of other Christians who talked about all the people they were leading to the Lord. He had never actually prayed with anyone to receive Jesus and had felt like a failure in that area. Amanda's testimony changed all that. He and Darci saw that just by doing what they were doing, telling their story and living their lives for Jesus, they were making a powerful impact on other people.

'Til We Meet Again

By the fall of 2011, Danny's father was having more and more difficulty breathing. He asked Danny one day, "Do you know what is great about you winning *The Biggest Loser?* You've done a great thing for the environment. Your 'carbon footprint' is much smaller!" Charlie's wit always reminded the family of one of his own heroes, Will Rogers.

Danny and Darci were just leaving a marriage seminar in Rome, Georgia, where they had been spending some time together, when Danny turned his phone on and saw that he had three messages: one from his mother, one from his sister Cathy, and one from his aunt. He felt dizzy. He knew something had happened to his father.

When he finally got in touch with Cathy, she sounded out-of-breath. "Danny, you need to come home." Pause. "He's gone, Danny."

211

Darci looked at Danny's ashen face and asked what was wrong. She was devastated to learn of Charlie's passing, because he had been the one who had embraced her as part of the family from the beginning of her relationship with Danny. He would call her at times and talk with her. He had sent her roses a few times on Mother's Day. Danny had told her that his dad had said to him, "You are lucky to have Darci as a wife. You'll realize that even more someday. She is a good wife."

In tears, they made one of the longest trips of their lives, knowing they were going home to bury a beloved father. Although he was a man of few words, when Charlie did speak it meant a lot and usually spoke volumes. He was shy and rarely expressed his emotions until his later years, but he was Danny's first hero, and that would never change. He taught him to be a man of honor, to work hard, to follow his heart, and to have faith that God would make everything work for his good.

After Charlie's funeral, they found a book Charlie had been filling out for David, a grandfather's book to his grandson. It asked Charlie questions about events in his life, growing up, things he liked, and more, so that David could know more about his grandfather. Charlie had completed half of it. As they read it, they found out things they had never known. It was like he was talking to them from Heaven. Then Danny read the question, "What is your favorite hymn?"

The answer: "'King of Kings,' by Danny Cahill."

Danny never doubted again that his father loved him and had been proud of him. Looking back, he could spot times in the past when his father was trying to tell him these things, but in his skewed, self-centered perspective, Danny could not receive the truth. He thanked God that now he could understand.

When Danny spoke at his father's funeral, he ended his words with "I've spent most of my life trying to make my father proud of me, and what I finally learned was that he is, and always was."

Danny cherishes all the years he fished, hunted, and surveyed thousands of miles of land with his father. He regrets that this horrible breathing disease took his life so soon, but at least his dad got to see him win *The Biggest Loser*, speak around the country, and write and play his music again. Danny would have loved to have taken his father with him to read his poetry. Although that cannot be, he and the rest of his family have the eternal comfort that someday they all will be together again. In the meantime, his father is freely breathing the fresh air in Heaven, surveying a much more magnificent land!

Genesis 50:20

Danny has been brought back to *The Biggest Loser* several times to inspire others. He continues to do television talk shows, and he speaks at motivational events for businesses and other organizations. He also speaks in churches, where he can freely share his faith. One of his favorite things, however, is when he and Darci tell their story together. Each time they share what is in their hearts, they are in awe of how God changes people's lives—and sometimes literally saves their lives—by using them and their story.

Someone will always ask Darci, "Why didn't you leave him?" Many have told her the gambling alone would have been the last straw, but certainly his weight and the way he treated her would have sent them packing.

She will say, "Love is a choice. It's not always an emotion or feeling. I made a commitment to Danny and to God. I want to keep my word. I've found when you honor God in your choices it comes back as a blessing to you. I chose to love Danny, even when it was really hard. When you live with an addict, you are faced with a lot of challenges! But I owed it to our kids and to us to choose to stay and fight for the love we had for each other."

They are honest about their continuing struggles in life, but now they can tell people to stay "real" with God and run to Him with everything that concerns them. They tell them how much He loves them and accepts them as they are. They also talk about staying connected in a fellowship of believers, because you can't grow and flourish without a good pastor and your brothers and sisters in the Lord. An honest, heartfelt relationship with God and His people is how Danny and Darci continue to mature and change together.

They are currently helping to design a seminar with friends called The Journey Training, which will incorporate much of what they have learned through the years. Their desire is to help individuals and couples who are struggling to see that who they are in Christ is enough, just like they were, as well as those who just want to make their lives better. They want to impart the life-changing truths, skills, and tools they have been given, so anyone who wants to can be the person they were created to be.

After *The Biggest Loser* ended, Danny and Darci began to receive hundreds of letters and cards from people who thanked them for being so transparent on the show, and that transparency continues as they travel and speak. Genesis 50:20, "You intended to harm me, but God intended it for good to accomplish what is now being done, the saving of many lives," is now a daily miracle in their lives.

A Final Word

Our lives have changed drastically for the better so many times, but it all began with giving our lives to Jesus Christ. We made our commitment to Him—to return His magnificent love and follow Him wherever He led us—back in those dark days of the chaos we had created for ourselves. Nothing was the same after that!

We soon learned that the commitment we made to Him might have been a one-time deal in terms of going to Heaven when we died, but it is a daily decision while we are here on earth. Sometimes, it is a moment-to-moment decision! One thing is absolutely certain: You would not be reading this book and we would not have written this book if we had never surrendered and continued to surrender our lives to Jesus.

Ultimately, our life was, is, and will be what we choose. The Bible says in Deuteronomy 30:19-20, "I have set before you life and death, blessings and curses. Now choose life, so that you and your children may live and that you may love the LORD your God, listen to his voice, and hold fast to him"(NIV). Every day we pray and set our hearts to choose life, to do the right thing. We don't always succeed, but in His love and grace we pick ourselves up, dust ourselves off, and continue to walk the path He has set before us.

We have doubted God. We have been betrayed, offended, and hurt by those we loved and trusted. We have gone through tragedy and heartache and wondered why God allowed it. We have screamed at Him and berated Him at times. But in each experience, we ultimately chose to love Him as He loved us, unconditionally, and to continue to follow Him. Thank God we did!

We realize now that every believer has to go through doubts, betrayal, hurt, offenses, tragedy, and anger. "Go through" means you choose to grow up and come out of it wiser and stronger. You turn to God instead of turning away from Him—no matter how you feel. And He never turns you away! NEVER! What's more, you receive more from Him than you ever could have imagined— and you learn about yourself. As we forgave others for betraying, hurting, and offending us, we realized that we also had betrayed, hurt, and offended others. Then we had to choose to receive forgiveness for our own faults and ask others to forgive us as well.

We also must choose to love and forgive ourselves. Jesus told us that all we need to do to live a great life is to love God with all our being and to love our neighbor as we love ourselves. We started out loving each other in a selfish, twisted way. Now we know that we can't really love anyone else in a healthy way if we don't first love and accept ourselves like Jesus loves and accepts us. This was and still is a big deal to us! Every day we try to remind each other and our children—and anyone God sends our way—how much God loves us all, and that we can and should love ourselves just as He does.

When we travel, people will ask us, "What is the most important thing you have learned in all this?" For us, it all boils down to this simple truth: If you lose the self-centered life and surrender to Jesus, you receive everything that is good and great. In Him, you gain it all!

So today, and every moment of every day, we choose Jesus.

Whoever loses their life for my sake will find it.

—Jesus of Nazareth

About the Authors

Danny is best known for winning season 8 of NBC's The Biggest Loser in 2009 and losing more weight than anyone in the history of the show. In 2008, he decided to change his direction in life to become the father and husband his family both desired and deserved. He set a goal to not only get chosen for the case of the show, but to win. Since achieving that seemingly impossible goal, losing 239 pounds in six and a half months, and winning the show, Danny has spoken all over the world at countless events and churches and companies. He is a motivator and an encourager. He has appeared on the television programs The Doctors, Larry King Live, NBC's Today Show, Suzie Orman, Live with Regis and Kelly, Issues with Jane Valez-Mitchell, and Praise the Lord. He has appeared on the national publications People Magazine, US Magazine, USA Today and Access Hollywood. His passion and purpose in life is to inspire people to overcome their situations and achieve their greatness through motivational speaking, television, writing music and authoring books. To find out more about Danny go to www.thedannycahill.com. Look for his music on iTunes and Amazon.com as well as his website.

Darci is a dedicated wife and mother. She has always had a passion for others, sometimes at the expense of her own needs. It seemed her prayers availed much for those around her, but she became discouraged when she did not see those fruits in her own life. When she felt that God told her to take care of her so she could then take care of others, the tide began to turn. When Danny left for The Biggest Loser, she stayed home to work, take care of the children and pay the bills. Not only did she achieve that, she continued to take care of herself and lost seventy pounds! Her purpose in life is to share the hope and abundance of Christ to every person that crosses her path. Her passion is to see everyone fufill their dreams and purpose in God. She continues to meet every week in the same prayer group that prayed that Danny find the passion to get on The Biggest Loser and regain his footing in life.

Danny and Darci now live with their children in Oklahoma. Their family is their first calling. Now they speak together spreading hope that marriages, lives, and dreams are never dead - they just need a little boost from God to get on their feet again.

PRAYER OF SALVATION

God loves you—no matter who you are, no matter what your past. God loves you so much that He gave His one and only begotten Son for you. The Bible tells us that "...whoever believes in Him shall not perish but have eternal life" (John 3:16 NIV). Jesus laid down His life and rose again so that we could spend eternity with Him in heaven and experience His absolute best on earth. If you would like to receive Jesus into your life, say the following prayer out loud and mean it from your heart.

Heavenly Father, I come to You admitting that I am a sinner. Right now, I choose to turn away from sin, and I ask You to cleanse me of all unrighteousness. I believe that Your Son, Jesus, died on the cross to take away my sins. I also believe that He rose again from the dead so that I might be forgiven of my sins and made righteous through faith in Him. I call upon the name of Jesus Christ to be the Savior and Lord of my life. Jesus, I choose to follow You and ask that You fill me with the power of the Holy Spirit. I declare that right now I am a child of God. I am free from sin and full of the righteousness of God. I am saved in Jesus' name. Amen.

If you prayed this prayer to receive Jesus Christ as your Savior for the first time, please contact us on the Web at **www.harrisonhouse.com** to receive a free book.

Or you may write to us at
Harrison House • P.O. Box 35035 • Tulsa, Oklahoma 74153

Fast. Easy.
Convenient.

For the latest Harrison House product information and author news, look no further than your computer. All the details on our powerful, life-changing products are just a click away. New releases, E-mail subscriptions, testimonies, monthly specials—find it all in one place. Visit harrisonhouse.com today!

harrisonhouse